UNITED IN PRAYER

UNITED IN PRAYER

Understanding and Praying the Lord's Prayer

PETER E. ROUSSAKIS

WIPF & STOCK · Eugene, Oregon

Wipf and Stock Publishers
199 W 8th Ave, Suite 3
Eugene, OR 97401

United in Prayer
By Roussakis, Peter E.
Copyright©2019 Apostolos
ISBN 13: 978-1-5326-8102-8
Publication date 2/2/2019
Previously published by Apostolos, 2019

All rights reserved. No part of this book may be reproduced or transmitted in any form or by any means, electronic or mechanical, including photocopying, recording, or by any information storage and retrieval system, without permission in writing from the publisher.

Unless otherwise indicated, Scripture references are taken from THE HOLY BIBLE, NEW INTERNATIONAL VERSION®, NIV® Copyright © 1973, 1978, 1984, 2011 by Biblica, Inc.® Used by permission. All rights reserved worldwide. British Library Cataloguing-in-Publication Data

Contents

Preface .... *vii*

CHAPTER ONE
Introducing the Lord's Prayer 1

CHAPTER TWO
Presenting an Overview 7

CHAPTER THREE
Noting the Jewish Setting 15

CHAPTER FOUR
Addressing God 25

CHAPTER FIVE
Hallowing God's Name 33

CHAPTER SIX
Entering God's Kingdom 43

CHAPTER SEVEN
Increasing in God's Kingdom 53

CHAPTER EIGHT
Imagining the Kingdom of God's Glory 61

CHAPTER NINE
Passing Into the Kingdom of God's Glory 71

CHAPTER TEN
Doing God's Will 81

CHAPTER ELEVEN
Depending on God..91

CHAPTER TWELVE
Requesting Daily Provisions...101

CHAPTER THIRTEEN
Seeking Forgiveness 109

CHAPTER FOURTEEN
Forgiving Others...121

CHAPTER FIFTEEN
Praying for Leniency..133

CHAPTER SIXTEEN
Pleading for Deliverance..141

CHAPTER SEVENTEEN
Praising God...151

CHAPTER EIGHTEEN
Summarizing the Lord's Prayer 157

CHAPTER NINETEEN
Praying the Lord's Prayer 169

Review Guide 181
Bibliography 187
Index..199
Biographical Note...206

Preface

Katelyn was thirteen when I was called as Pastor of the First Brethren Church of Burlington, Indiana. She had been suffering from a disease called ulcerative colitis which necessitated her being in the hospital periodically to receive medications and blood transfusions. It was a hard road for a young teenager. Some five years later, her condition worsened significantly. In great pain, she was rushed to the hospital. While in the emergency room, her spiritual reflex action was to pray the Lord's Prayer. She did so, over and over and over. Finally her circumstances stabilized well enough to prepare her for surgery to remove her large intestine. The surgery was successful, leaving her with a colostomy. Fortunately after several months, it was possible to reverse it, and she is doing very well.

Katey could have prayed her own prayers. However, to her it seemed to be a desperately important moment in her life, and the Lord's Prayer, *the* prayer of prayers for the Christian, was the prayer through which her most urgent pleas could be expressed. Later Katey said she appreciated so much my series of fourteen sermons on the Lord's Prayer. She said: "You're getting through." Praying the Lord's Prayer gave her strength to cope, trust in God, and to go on.

Christians everywhere, whatever their denominational or non-denominational stripe, are uniquely linked together by "the tie that binds our hearts in Christian love." That tie, Jesus Christ, provided disciples with instruction on how to pray and what to say. Praying together the prayer he taught contributes to the binding of our hearts, and provides a prayer which is so sacred for the Christian, that in times of trial as well as ease, we may turn to God through the praying of *the* prayer the Savior provided for his followers.

UNITED IN PRAYER

The overall objectives herein include contributing to the 'binding' through an understanding of Jesus' timely instruction, and through intentional, meaningful praying of the Lord's Prayer in public worship. Moreover, to offer parishioners a greater awareness and deeper knowledge of the truths encapsulated in the prayer, and to assist pastors and teachers in their ministries of preaching and teaching on this subject, this volume is offered.

For those Christian communities where the Lord's Prayer is prayed regularly in worship, it is likely that many parishioners are unaware of the full meanings of each of the phrases of the prayer; thus the need for pastors to provide instruction, that the prayer may have its greatest impact in the lives of those who utilize it in private and corporate devotion. Upon examination of the phrases of the prayer, which forms the greater body of this volume, it will be seen that contained in these five verses of scripture, Matthew 6:9-13, the version most commonly used throughout Christendom, there is a goldmine of truth, a mini-encyclopedia of Christian belief; and, therefore, when we pray the Lord's Prayer, we as Christians are not merely praying the prayer Jesus taught, we are in a fashion affirming the truths contained within the preface, the petitions, and the closing statement of praise of the prayer. Not only so, Christians are united, if not in all ways, at least in prayer, and in particular in the praying of the Lord's Prayer. Unity through learning and praying are worthy endeavors, to which this volume is dedicated.

Before presenting an explication of the prayer's meanings, especially for those who would like to pursue deeper study of this "Prayer of prayers," an *Introduction* to major sources of study of the prayer is presented, followed by an *Overview* of the prayer's scriptural context, inclusions and order, and then an introduction to appreciating the *Jewish Setting* of the prayer. The concluding chapter of the work will again take up the theme of Christians being united through learning about the prayer and praying it together, and through a consideration of the various potentialities of praying the prayer. It is the desire of this writer that through the content, reading and application of these pages the work of God may be advanced.

P.E.R., Burlington, Indiana, Spring 2007

CHAPTER ONE
Introducing the Lord's Prayer

Our Father in heaven,
hallowed be your name,
your kingdom come,
your will be done
on earth as it is in heaven.
Give us today our daily bread.
Forgive us our debts,
as we also have forgiven our debtors.
And lead us not into temptation,
but deliver us from the evil one.
(Matt. 6:9-13 NIV)

Since the early church, Christians have been praying the Lord's Prayer in public worship. Thomas Aquinas (c.1225-1274) referred to it as the best of all prayers.[1] Nicolas Ayo described the prayer as seminal of all Christian prayer.[2] In the opening remarks of his comprehensive work on the Lord's Prayer, Thomas Watson (1620-1688) described Jesus' words as a "directory for prayer" and a "system or body of divinity."[3] Most Christians, we would think, would resonate affirmatively with the idea of the prayer being a directory or outline for appropriate prayer. The notion of the Lord's Prayer being an outline for Christian prayer has been accepted generally. John Calvin (1509-1564) referred to it as "a prescribed form."[4] Martin Luther (1483-1546) called

---

[1] Thomas Acquinas. *Summa Theologiae* Vol. 39 (New York: McGraw-Hill Book Company, 1964), II, II, 83, 9.

[2] Nicolas Ayo. *The Lord's Prayer: A Survey Theological and Literary* (Notre Dame, Indiana: University of Notre Dame, 1992), 6.

[3] Thomas Watson. *The Lord's Prayer* (Edinburgh: The Banner of Truth Trust, 1993), 1.

[4] John T. McNeill, ed. *Calvin: Institutes of the Christian Religion* (Philadelphia: The Westminster Press, 1960), Vol. 2, III, XX, 34.

it "a brief formula" for prayer.[5] Matthew Henry (1662-1714) described it as "a method for praying."[6] More contemporary labels include Frank Stagg's traditional "Model Prayer,"[7] David Jeremiah's "road map for prayer,"[8] and Max Lucado's "floor plan to our spiritual house."[9]

The other remark by Watson, that the Lord's Prayer is "a system or body of divinity," may not be understood or appreciated fully by parishioners of any tradition unless a series of sermons or classes were offered explaining the meaning of each phrase of the prayer. Through such ways it may bring to peoples' awareness a dimension of the prayer not previously considered. Indeed, presenting such a consideration is another purpose of this study.

This second remark of Watson's was based on the truth of the prayer's composition and upon a statement of Tertullian (c.150-220), who, in his treatise *De Oratione* ("On Prayer"), called the Lord's Prayer a "compendium of the whole gospel" *(breviarium totius evangelii)*.[10] Other commentators have spoken similarly. Cyprian (200-258) said the Lord's Prayer is a "comprehensive and sublime compend."[11] Luther characterized the trilogy of the Catechism (the Ten Commandments, the Creed, and the Lord's Prayer), as a "digest of doctrine."[12] G.

---

[5] Martin Luther. "The Sermon on the Mount: Sermons," *Luther's Works* Vol. 21, Jaroslav Pelikan, ed. (St. Louis: Concordia Publishing House, 1956), 145

[6] Matthew Henry. *Matthew Henry's Commentary On the Whole Bible* Vol. 5 (Peabody, Mass: Hendrickson Publishers, 1994), 59.

[7] Frank Stagg. "Matthew," *The Broadman Bible Commentary* Vol. 8 (Nashville: Broadman Press, 1969), 115.

[8] David Jeremiah. *Prayer The Great Adventure* (Sisters, Oregon: Multnomah Publishers, Inc.), 69.

[9] Max Lucado. *The Great House of God* (Dallas: Word Publishing, 1997), 7.

[10] Watson, 1. "Compendium" is Watson's and Ayo's (p.5) rendering of Tertullian's "breviarium." "An epitome of the whole Gospel" is the translation given by the Rev. S. Thelwall in *Ante-Nicene Fathers*, Vol. 3, Alexander Roberts & James Donaldson, eds. (Peabody, Mass: Hendrickson Publishers, 1994), 681.

[11] Cyprian. "Elucidation III," *Ante-Nicene Fathers* Vol.5, Alexander Roberts and James Donaldson, eds. (Peabody, Mass: Henrickson Publishers, 1994), 559.

[12] F. Samuel Janzow. *Luther's Large Catechism* (St. Louis: Concordia Publishing House, 1978), 12.

Campbell Morgan (1863-1945) described the prayer as being a part of the "Manifesto of the King,"[13] referring to the Sermon on the Mount of which the Lord's Prayer is a part in Matthew's Gospel. William Willimon and Stanley Hauerwas call it "public theology."[14] In Philip Schaff's (1819-1893) *A Christian Catechism for Sunday Schools and Families* (1880), the famous church historian described the Lord's Prayer as "the gospel in a nutshell."[15] And Nicolas Ayo commented: "The Lord's Prayer is a precis of the whole gospel, the distillation of the substance of the good news."[16]

Individual works which masterfully dissect the phrases of the Lord's Prayer, and which thereby attest to the prayer as saturated with doctrine, include Nicolas' Ayo's work (1992). Karl Barth's (1886-1968) treatise, *Prayer*, originally published in 1949, is a most interesting and valuable commentary on the prayer from the view of the Protestant Reformers. Thomas Watson's work mentioned above provides a thorough explication of every phrase of the prayer. Other recent volumes listed in the bibliography provide interesting insight. Few, however, are comprehensive; thus one justification for this study.

We may say, therefore, that the Lord's Prayer contains an *encapsulation of Christian belief*. Because it does, it serves as an outline for and a potential source, when explicated as such, of a significant body of Christian doctrine. Moreover, a logical deduction is that the text of the Lord's Prayer serves Christians in worship as one unique and readily accessible confession of faith. While the Lord's Prayer is not a creed in a formal sense of the term, because it is an arrangement of specific theological themes and concerns, it has confessional import. Needless to say, however, the text by itself would be of little value as a confession of faith unless it were prayed, unless the text were recited and of course

---

[13] G. Campbell Morgan. *The Practice of Prayer* (Belfast, Northern Ireland: Ambassador Productions, Ltd, 1995), 57.

[14] William H. Willimon and Stanley Hauerwas. *Lord, Teach Us: The Lord's Prayer and the Christian Life* (Nashville: Abingdon Press, 1996), 17.

[15] Philip Schaff. *A Christian Catechism for Sunday Schools and Families* (Philadelphia: American Sunday School Union, 1880), 29.

[16] Ayo, 6.

believed. Again, more than merely enabling the community to offer a common prayer to God, because the Lord's Prayer is a compendium of the Gospel, praying it together in the corporate worship setting may be thought of as a way the community of faith professes its faith and is unified, a position taken by J. Harold Ellens in his "Communication Theory and Petitionary Prayer,"[17] which will be highlighted in the closing chapter.

In addition to those mentioned above, a number of other sources are worthy of note, resources which reflect this writers suggestions for further study and which have contributed to the writing of the present volume. They include the commentaries of John Calvin, William Barclay, Matthew Henry, and Frank Stagg. Two collections of articles are especially valuable. *The Lord's Prayer and Other Prayer Texts from the Greco-Roman Era*, edited by Princeton Seminary's James H. Charlesworth, provides an extensive bibliography. The other is *The Lord's Prayer and Jewish Liturgy*, edited by Jakob Petuchowski, Research Professor of Jewish Theology and Liturgy at Hebrew Union College, and Michael Brocke, Professor of Judaic Studies at the University of Regensburg, Germany, in which is found a number of essays originally delivered at an inter-denominational conference in Freiburg im Breisgau, Germany in 1973 sponsored by the Oration Dominica Foundation. The topic for discussion was the Lord's Prayer, with the objective of identifying the common affirmations of Christians and Jews which underlie the prayer. Of the inclusions in this collection, Jean Carmignac's "The Spiritual Wealth of the Lord's Prayer" is significant because the reader is introduced to Carmignac's *Reserches sur le Notre Pere* in which he provided over eighty pages of bibliography on the subject.

Also included in the Petuchowski and Brocke volume is Josef Bommer's "The Lord's Prayer in Pastoral Usage," which explores what could be termed the ministry of the Lord's Prayer in the parish. Herbert Jochum's "Teaching the Lord's Prayer" brings to the reader's attention the role the prayer has played in catechetical instruction and

---

[17] J. Harold Ellens. "Communication Theory and Petitionary Prayer," *Journal of Psychology and Theology* Vol. 5, no. 1 (1977): 48-54.

how it may be used in today's churches in relevant fashion.

More popular works which offer interesting insights include Brian Dodd's *Praying Jesus' Way* (1997), a collection of sermons. David Jeremiah's *Prayer the Great Adventure* (1997) discusses the Lord's Prayer as a means of teaching what the Bible says about prayer in general. In Max Lucado's *The Great House of God* (1997) the author compares the Christian's spiritual life to the care of the rooms of a house, each one described in terms of one of the phrases of Jesus' prayer. The two offerings by Kenneth Stevenson, *Abba Father: Understanding and Using the Lord's Prayer* (2000) and *The Lord's Prayer: A Text in Tradition* (2004), are masterful. Additional volumes are listed in the bibliography.

Chapter Two
Presenting an Overview

A thirty second silence turned into a vocal recitation of The Lord's Prayer at a graduation ceremony. Prayer had long been a tradition during commencements at Northern High School in Silver Spring, Maryland. Senior Julie Schenk planned to deliver an invocation at the May 26, 1999 event, but fellow student Nick Becker objected, saying prayer is inappropriate at a public ceremony. The state attorney general's office agreed with a request by the American Civil Liberties Union on Becker's behalf. It informed Calvert County officials that graduation prayers violate the constitutional separation of church and state. As a compromise, Schenk agreed to ask for a thirty second "time for reflection" that did not mention God. But God was mentioned nevertheless. A man in the crowd began to recite The Lord's Prayer aloud after Schenk began the moment of silence. Virtually the entire 4000 member audience, including many students, joined in, the Associated Press reported... "This is a church-going community, and no one in Annapolis or Washington, D.C. is going to tell us when and where we can pray," said Linda Kelley, president of the Calvert County Commission who joined in the prayer. "The school administrators did the legal thing and complied with the law. But the audience took this one over."[18]

The people couldn't help themselves (or rather they did). They made a statement. Prayer is a natural and important part of human life and particularly the Christian's life. People instinctively have a need for touch with God, especially at very significant moments in their lives. Martin Luther, the great sixteenth century

---

[18] This incident was reported over the internet in the June 1, 1999 *Religion Today* news summary.

reformer, said: "To be a Christian without prayer is no more possible than to be alive without breathing."[19] Just as we breathe air to be sustained physically, so also Christian's pray as a part of being spiritually alive. James Montgomery (1771-1854), the nineteenth century author of the hymn, "Prayer is the Soul's Sincere Desire," wrote in stanza four: Prayer is the Christian's vital breath, the Christian's native air...

Certainly it is intended that in prayer we acknowledge our dependence upon God, giving him the glory, and affording us an inner assurance that God is able to care for and direct our lives. Luther said: "I have so much to do that I must spend the first three hours of each day in prayer."[20]

As with any behavior, prayer is learned. Not all Christians are comfortable praying in public. They may not know what to say or how to say it. While silence can be an integral part of intentionally entering into the presence of God, being still, listening as it were to the thoughts God may arouse within us, prayer, whether in public or in private, is talking to God, entering into a reverent fellowship with God, speaking words of praise, confession, and petition. To be sure, if guidance was available from the scriptures on how to pray, Christians would want to avail themselves of that instruction. Of course such direction was given by Jesus himself. In the New Testament two versions of the Lord's Prayer are provided, one in Matthew 6:9-13, and the other in Luke 11:2-4. Whereas settings of the Matthean version have become the ones in common use worldwide, we shall base our remarks primarily on that version, with an occasional reference to Luke's. In this chapter we present an overview of the prayer, which, as illustrated by the graduation audience mentioned above, is a powerful symbol of and vehicle for *unifying* believers, for *communicating* with God, and for *affirming* our faith in God, upon whom we are dependent for all things.

---

[19] Quoted in George Sweeting. *Who Said That?* (Chicago: Moody Press, 1995), 359.

[20] Michael P. Green, ed. *Illustrations for Biblical Preaching* (Grand Rapids: Baker Book House, 1989), 277.

The Context

In order to fully appreciate the meaning of the prayer, it is appropriate to consider the context within which Jesus' prayer was spoken; namely, chapters five, six and seven of Matthew's Gospel which record what is called Jesus' "Sermon on the Mount." Because in the Lukan account (Lk. 6:20-49) the Sermon on the Mount follows the calling of the disciples, the Sermon has been viewed as a kind of ordination address. From Matthew it becomes clearer that the Sermon may not be a sermon at all, but rather a collection of the primary sayings of Jesus. John Calvin described the Sermon as "...a brief summary of the doctrine of Christ...collected out of his many and various discourses..."[21] In similar fashion the Sermon has been called a "Compendium of Christ's Doctrine," "The Magna Charta of the Kingdom," and "The Manifesto of the King."[22] If one were to search for the core of Jesus' thought and instruction, the Sermon on the Mount would be the material to examine.

Included in this collection of the theology of Jesus are the Beatitudes, those statements which refer to the blessedness of those who exemplify Godly dispositions. "Blessed are the pure in heart, for they shall see God" (Mt. 5:8) is one example. Also included in the Sermon on the Mount are the Similitudes: "You are the salt of the earth...You are the light of the world..."(5:13-16). The Golden Rule (7:12), "So in everything, do to others what you would have them do to you, for this sums up the Law and the Prophets," is a part of this collection of the teachings of Jesus. His instruction and interpretation of the meaning of the law is a part of this body of divinity as well. It is within this particular context that the Lord's Prayer is located. It was Martin Luther's view that in the Sermon on the Mount Jesus wanted to expose and oppose all false teaching and provide the true meaning

---

[21] John Calvin. "Commentary and Harmony of the Evangelists," *Calvin's Commentaries* Vol. XVI (Grand Rapids: Baker Book House, 1993), 259.

[22] William Barclay. *The Gospel of Matthew* Vol. 1, rev. ed. (Philadelphia: The Westminster Press, 1975), 84.

of the scriptures.[23] This becomes very evident in Matthew 6.

What lies behind Jesus' remarks in this sixth chapter is the importance to the Jew of performing three essential acts of righteousness: almsgiving (that is, giving to the needy, 6:2-4), praying (6:5-15), and fasting (6:16-18). Jesus instructed the disciples not to go about doing these things in the way "the hypocrites do in the synagogues and on the streets" (6:2), an obvious criticism of the Pharisees who took great pleasure, it seemed, in announcing their deeds.

> When you give to the needy do not let your left hand know what your right hand is doing, so that your giving may be in secret. Then your Father, who sees what is done in secret, will reward you (6:3).

> When you fast do not look somber as the hypocrites do, for they disfigure their faces to show men they are fasting. I tell you the truth, they have received their reward in full. But when you fast, put oil on your head and wash your face, so it will not be obvious to men that you are fasting, but only to your Father, who is unseen; and your Father, who sees what is done in secret, will reward you (6:16-18).

> And when you pray do not be like the hypocrites, for they love to pray standing in the synagogues and on the street corners to be seen by men. I tell you the truth, they have received their reward in full. But when you pray, go to your room, close the door and pray to your Father, who is unseen. Then your Father, who sees what is done in secret, will reward you. And when you pray do not keep on babbling like pagans, for they think they will be heard because of their many words. Do not be like them, for your Father knows what you need before you ask him (6:5-8).

---

[23] Martin Luther. *Luther's Works* Vol. 21, 3.

What is presented by Jesus in Matthew 6, therefore, is a discourse on having the proper motive for one's acts of righteousness. Practicing piety should not be thought of as mere outward performance, because such expression can come from an ungodly motive as well as from a God-honoring intention.[24] The necessity of a "purity of intention,"[25] as John Wesley (1703-1791) put it, is the main point Jesus was making in this body of instruction, and is the context of Jesus' prayer as presented in Matthew's record.

The Inclusions

Following the criticism of insincere religiosity, Jesus provided the disciples with instruction on how to pray and what kinds of matters to include in a well-intended prayer. An appropriate prayer should begin by addressing God, such as: "Our Father who art in heaven." The prayer should acknowledge that we who pray desire to honor God in our lives: "Hallowed be thy name." The disciples were instructed to pray for the fulfillment of the general plan of God, thinking of the work and welfare of God first before making personal requests, as in: "Thy kingdom come. Thy will be done on earth as it is in heaven." Petitions for basic needs then may follow, acknowledging therein our dependence upon God for all things: "Give us this day our daily bread." God's forgiveness for sin should be sought, expecting that if we forgive the sins others may have committed against us, then God will forgive ours: "Forgive us our debts as we forgive our debtors." Then it is important to seek God's protection against the forces of evil which can so easily cause us to stray from the path of righteousness: "And lead us not into temptation, but deliver us from the evil one." In the KJV and the

---

[24] Luther described the hypocrites mentioned by Jesus as those who "imagined that their life was satisfactory and good if only they did [good] works, contributed alms generously, fasted, and prayed, regardless of how their heart stood in relation to God. In addition, they were polluted by the filthy habit of doing it all to have the people see them and give them honor and glory for it." *Luther's Works* Vol. 21, 131.

[25] John Wesley. "Upon Our Lord's Sermon on the Mount," Sermon XXVI, Discourse VI, *The Works of John Wesley*, third edition, Vol. V (Grand Rapids: Baker Book House, 1991), 328.

NKJV the traditional doxological closing of the prayer is given: "For thine is the kingdom, and the power, and the glory, forever. Amen" (KJV). In the oldest available manuscripts of the Bible which translators use, this closing expression of praise is not included. This enables us to understand why in the NIV and other versions there is no closing doxology. However, there seems to be nothing improper in utilizing it. Indeed, it's inclusion in later manuscripts suggests the early church considered a closing appropriate.

The Order

In this initial examination of how the disciples were instructed to pray, we should note the order of the inclusions. It begins with a preface: "Our Father who art in heaven." The preface serves as an introduction, an invocation, a "solemn address".[26] The preface is followed by two groups of petitions. The first deals with divine matters, while the second group is concerned with human needs. The first three petitions are directed Godward. They have to do with God and his rightful place in the world. They may be more clearly understood by rendering them as the following:

May your name be kept holy.
May your kingdom come.
May your will be done on earth as in heaven.

The second group of three petitions deals with human needs: daily necessities, forgiveness of sins, and fortitude in the face of trial and temptation. As creatures of time we humans are dependent fully upon God's supply for all our days; in the past, as exemplified in the request for forgiveness; in the present, by the need for regular provisions; and in the future, as inner strength will be needed when facing evils which can sidetrack believers.

When we think about the whole of our lives, as William Barclay (1907-1978) reflects, we realize that the prayer takes into consideration the extent of God's personhood and concern. For "daily bread" in the

---

[26] Matthew Henry. *Matthew Henry's Commentary On the Whole Bible* Vol. 5, 59.

present we request of God the Father, our Caregiver. When we seek forgiveness, our request is made with the belief that Jesus, God the Son, died as the atonement for our sins. And when we ask for protection against temptation and evil we realize that it is God the Holy Spirit, our Comforter, Guide, and Guardian, who will be with us. Jesus taught his disciples to bring all of life to the fullness of God's personhood.[27]

In sum, the Lord's Prayer begins with a *preface* followed by six *petitions*. It closes with a statement of *praise* ascribing to God the honor he is worthy of receiving from his creatures. Whatever we include in the middle of our prayers, we should begin and end them with expressions which give glory to God. The Lord's Prayer is *the Prayer of prayers*, the most excellent of Christian prayers, a prayer to pray and a model for all our prayers, which is why many Christian communities pray it regularly in public worship. Whereas the Ten Commandments provide a rule for life, and creeds give a faithful summary of Christian belief, the Lord's Prayer is Jesus' prescription for praying. It is comprehensive in that it says much in a few words; it is clear, direct, plain and intelligible; and it is complete, for it contains the primary things that we need to ask and that God can bestow.[28]

Simply put, whereas prayer puts us in touch with God so that we will know how to live, how to think and act in a Godly fashion, so also the Lord's Prayer puts us in touch with God, revealing to us what to believe, and leading us how to behave.

---

[27] Barclay, *The Gospel of Matthew*, Vol. 1, 199-200.
[28] Thomas Watson. *The Lord's Prayer*, 2.

CHAPTER THREE

Noting the Jewish Setting

Before we begin the exploration of the beliefs which are suggested by the preface, petitions, and the closing praise of Jesus' prayer, and in order to be thorough in our appreciation of its contents, we will discuss briefly the Jewish matrix from which the Lord's Prayer was spawned.

Intention

The most obvious matter to note first regarding the Jewish setting of the prayer is that which we observe from the Lukan account. "One day Jesus was praying in a certain place. When he finished, one of his disciples said to him, 'Lord, teach us to pray just as John taught his disciples'" (Lk. 11:1). On this William Barclay commented: "It was the regular custom for a Rabbi to teach his disciples a simple prayer which they might habitually use. John had done that for his disciples, and now Jesus' disciples came asking him to do the same for them."[29] The custom in Jesus' day was for a Rabbi to teach his followers a prayer which was of his composition and would be uniquely theirs to pray. It was a *mark of identity* with that particular Rabbi. This *intention* is the most conspicuous evidence of the Jewish setting of the prayer.

Content

Secondly, the *content* of the prayer is indicative of Old Testament Jewish thought. Without elaboration, a few examples of content parallels include God as Father (Isa. 63:16), God's Name (Ex. 20:7, 2 Sam. 6:2, Jer. 7:10-11), the doing of God's will (Ps. 119:30-33), God's provision for daily bread (Ex. 16:14-21), God's forgiveness (Ps. 130:4, and throughout the Old Testament), God's protection (Ps. 91:14, Pr. 2:8), God's deliverance (1 Sam. 12:10, Ps. 3:8, Ps. 32:7), and God's praise (1

---

[29] William Barclay. *The Gospel of Luke*, rev. ed. (Philadelphia: The Westminster Press, 1975), 143.

Chr. 29:10-13, Dan. 2:20, the Psalms). Because of the ideational connection of the Lord's Prayer with Old Testament thought, Kenneth Stevenson has referred to the Lord's Prayer as a "canonical prayer."[30]

Shape and Direction

A further correspondence with Jewish piety is the *shape* of the Lord's Prayer echoed in other Old Testament inclusions. The *Shema* (Deut. 6:4-5) served the Jews as a confession of faith.[31] "Its threefold sequence of heart, soul and strength could have inspired the 'twice threefold' arrangement of [Jesus'] own prayer given to the disciples."[32] Most certainly Jesus, as all Jews, would have recited/prayed the *Shema* twice daily.[33]

The twofold *direction* of the Lord's Prayer with the first three petitions being directed God-ward, and the second group of three focusing on human concerns, is similar to that of the Ten Commandments; the first four Commandments speaking of respect and duty to God, while the remaining six emphasize regard and duty to others. It is worth noting this two-part direction and movement is seen as well in the Beatitudes (Mt. 5:3-12). In content, shape, and direction of thought, the Lord's Prayer echoes the Jewish piety of the Old Testament era, piety which was also a part of Jewish life in Jesus' day.

---

[30] Kenneth Stevenson. *Abba Father: Understanding and Using the Lord's Prayer* (Harrisburg, Penn: Morehouse Publishing, 2000), 12.

[31] Emil Schurer, *A History of the Jewish People in the Time of Jesus Christ* Second Division, Vol. III (Peabody, Mass: Hendrikson Publishers, Inc., 1995 edition), 84; and Jakob J. Petuchowski, "The Liturgy of the Synagogue," *The Lord's Prayer and Jewish Liturgy*, Jakob J. Petuchowski and Michael Brocke, eds. (New York: The Seabury Press, 1978), 49-50.

[32] Stevenson, *Abba Father*, 36.

[33] Schurer, 84, and Petuchowski, "The Liturgy of the Synagogue," 48-50. In the morning the *Shema* was recited preceded by two benedictions (Heb. *berakoth*) and followed by one benediction. These are 'blessing' prayers, as in "Blessed are You, O Lord...". The *Shema* was also recited in the evening preceded by two benedictions and followed by two more. Because the *Shema* does not stand alone in these ways, it is appropriate to say the *Shema* is *prayed*. While Jewish liturgy has no creed as do Christians who recite the Apostles' or Nicene creeds or other statements of faith, the 'Shema and Its Blessings' functions in that role in synagogue worship.

Prayer Tradition

Another major area with which the Lord's Prayer has similarities is the Jewish prayer tradition of the synagogue. A quote from G. Campbell Morgan will serve to introduce this.

> It has been affirmed and correctly so that [the Lord's Prayer] is not a new prayer. Its every petition is to be found in the Talmudic writings... There can be little doubt... that the men who heard the Master, when He first gave them the prayer, were familiar with all its petitions. In all probability they had used them constantly in their worship from childhood... [Jesus] gathers together the things with which they were most familiar and placed them in such perfect relation to each other as to reveal as never before the whole plane of prayer.[34]

Two things upon which we shall comment from Morgan's quote are the 'Talmudic writings' and 'their worship'.

The *Talmud* was written between the third and sixth centuries CE. Its significance is that it is the written record of accumulated Jewish oral tradition of theological import as far back as 450 BCE. After many hundreds of years of oral transmission, the teachings of Rabbis were put into print. We in the Christian tradition might think of the Talmud (meaning study or learning) as a commentary on and application of the Torah (law/instruction), the first five books of the Old Testament. In the Talmud all aspects of Jewish life are discussed.[35] In it there is a record of Jewish liturgical memory, and it is this material which has par-

---

[34] G. Campbell Morgan. *The Practice of Prayer*, 59.

[35] The Talmud (study/learning), which overall is a commentary on Torah (law/instruction), has two parts. The first is the Mishnah (repeated study) which is the written record of many centuries of oral commentary on the law. Such oral commentary was memorized by repetition (repeated study). It is a systematized collection of the Oral Law of the Old Testament as well as the political and civil laws of Judaism, traced as far back as 450 BCE. The second part of the Talmud is the Gemara (completed study) which, after Mishnah was recorded, included written explanations and commentary on Mishnah. Gemara contains rabbinic discussions, explanations and amplifications of the content of Mishnah.

ticular bearing on the present consideration of the Lord's Prayer's Jewish setting. As we shall see, what Jesus offered may very well have been a condensed version of other Jewish prayers which he and his disciples and all other devout Jews would have prayed publicly in the Temple and synagogue as well as in private devotions. There would have been a familiarity with the phrases of the Lord's Prayer. The disciples would have grasped the significance of them, and they would have been easily remembered.

Moreover, it is also known from the Talmud that "it was customary for prominent masters to recite brief prayers of their own in addition to the regular prayers of worship; and there is indeed a certain similarity noticeable between these prayers and that of Jesus."[36] What were some of the Jewish prayers upon which the above statements have their basis?

Two prayers included in synagogue worship with which the Lord's Prayer possesses parallel aspects are the *Kaddish* and the *Amidah*.[37]

---

[36] Kaufmann Kohler, "The Lord's Prayer." An internet generated article from the Jewish Encyclopedia.com. The Talmudic parallels he cites are Tosef., Ber. iii. 7; Ber. 16b.-17a., 29b; Yer. Ber. iv. 7d.

[37] Other prayers could be cited and discussed, for there are other parallels in Jewish liturgical and devotional tradition. However, the Kaddish and the Amidah are most often cited and are sufficient for our present purposes. One of the scholarly sources for understanding the Jewish setting of the Lord's Prayer and its parallels from Jewish prayer tradition is the one mentioned in Chapter One and in note 31, *The Lord's Prayer and Jewish Liturgy*, edited by Jakob Petuchowski and Michael Brocke. In this goldmine of material it is worth noting the contributions by Alfons Deissler, "The Spirit of the Lord's Prayer in the Faith and Worship of the Old Testament" (3-17); Jakob J. Petuchowski, "Jewish Prayer Texts of the Rabbinic Period" (21-43) and "The Liturgy of the Synagogue" (45-57); Baruch Graubard, "The Kaddish Prayer" (59-72); Simon Lauer, "Abhinu Malkenu: Our Father, Our King!" (73-79); Joseph Heinemann, "The Background of Jesus' Prayer in the Jewish Liturgical Tradition" (81-89); Gordon J. Bahr, "The Use of the Lord's Prayer in the Primitive Church" (149-155); Michael Brocke, "The Liturgies of Synagogue and Church. An Introduction" (205-220). Other sources of information regarding the Jewish setting of the Lord's Prayer include *Elucidations III* of Cyprian; James H. Charlesworth, "Jewish Prayers in the Time of Jesus," *Princeton Seminary Bulletin* Supplement 2 (1992): 36-55; and Brad H. Young, *The Jewish Background to the Lord's Prayer* (Austin, TX: Center for Judaic-Christian Studies, 1984).

Noting the Jewish Setting

According to Kenneth Stevenson, the Kaddish, which is Aramaic for "holy" referring to the praise of God, has occurred in various versions. For example, appearing in a prayer book, *Seder Tefillot*, compiled in the ninth century CE, the text of the Kaddish reads (with similarities to the Lord's Prayer in italics added):

Exalted and sanctified be His great Name.

In the world which He created *according to His will,* may *He establish His kingdom* in your lifetime, and in the lifetime of the entire House of Israel, speedily and soon.

May *His great Name be blessed for ever and to all eternity.*

Praised, glorified, exalted, extolled, revered, highly honored and adored is the Name of the Holy One, blessed be He beyond all the blessings, hymns, praises and consolations that are ever uttered in the world.[38]

Settings of the Kaddish longer than this example were used by the synagogue preacher at the close of his exposition of scripture and at eulogies for the deceased. A Kaddish may also be used by the congregation in response to the synagogue preacher's sermon. Shorter versions were used by devout Jews in their daily private prayers[39] as in the following (italics added):

Exalted and hallowed be His great Name in the world which He created *according to His will. May He establish His kingdom* in your days, and in the lifetime of the whole household of Israel, speedily and at a near time. Amen.[40]

---

[38] Kenneth W. Stevenson, *The Lord's Prayer: A Text in Tradition* (Minneapolis: Fortress Press, 2004), 26. The above example and the one to follow are referred to as "Half-Kaddish" because it is briefer than the longer "Full-Kaddish" which has additional expressions of praise.

[39] Stevenson, *Abba Father*, 56-57.

[40] Petuchowski, "Jewish Prayer Texts of the Rabbinic Period," 37.

Baruch Graubard describes the Kaddish as "one of the most frequently repeated prayers in the traditional synagogue service… That prayer is the doxology *par excellence* of the synagogue liturgy…"[41]

The second Jewish prayer with which the Lord's Prayer has parallels is commonly referred to as the *Amidah* (standing) because of the posture of the worshipers when it is prayed. The Amidah is more specifically called the Eighteen Benedictions *(Shemone Esre Berakoth)* which were a part of the daily synagogue service. The Hebrew word translated *benedictions* is *berakoth*. It may also be rendered *eulogies* or *blessings*. In Jewish liturgy a benediction is a prayer which begins or ends with 'You are praised, O Lord', 'Blessed be Thou, O Lord', or 'Blessed are You…'. The Amidah and the 'Shema and Its Blessings'[42] together serve as two central units of the synagogue service.[43] Every devout Jew is expected to pray these prayers in their daily private prayers as well.

In the Talmud the sacred memories of the origins of the Amidah going back to the prophets are included.[44] The first three of the blessings of the Amidah are expressions of praise. The greater number, four through fifteen, are petitions, which explains why the Amidah is additionally referred to as *Tefillah* (The Prayer).[45] Tefillah is petitionary prayer, the basic Jewish form of prayer.[46] The last three benedictions are again expressions of praise and thanksgiving. The following are examples from the Amidah which are paralleled in the Lord's Prayer.[47]

---

[41] Graubard, "The Kaddish Prayer," 59.

[42] See note 33 above.

[43] Petuchowski, "The Liturgy of the Synagogue," 55.

[44] Rabbi Lawrence A. Hoffman, ed., *My People's Prayer Book: Traditional Prayers, Modern Commentaries* Volume 2, The Amidah (Woodstock, Vermont: Jewish Lights Publishing, 2003), 21.

[45] Ibid., 11.

[46] Alfons Deissler described the Lord's Prayer as 'biblical tefillah' in "The Spirit of the Lord's Prayer," 4.

[47] The examples are from Jakob Petuchowski, "Jewish Prayer Texts of the Rabbinic Period," 30-34.

Noting the Jewish Setting

Our Father is present in benedictions five and six. Benediction six begins:

Let us return, our Father, unto Your Torah.

Hallowed be thy Name is echoed in the third benediction.

Holy are You and holy is Your Name;
and holy ones praise You everyday.
You are praised, O Lord, the holy God.

The themes of *Thy kingdom come, thy will be done* are found in benedictions eleven through fourteen. The fourteenth includes:

Return in mercy to Jerusalem, Your city.
Dwell in it, as You have promised.
Rebuild it soon in our days as an
  everlasting building; and speedily
  set up in it the throne of David.
You are praised, O Lord, Builder of Jerusalem.

The provision for *bread* is heard in benediction nine.

Bless this year for us, O Lord our God,
  and all the varieties of its produce for good.
Grant blessings upon the face of the earth,
  and satiate us out of Your goodness.
Bless our year like the good years.
You are praised, O Lord, who blesses the years.

Benediction thirteen speaks of the security of God's people as in the *lead us* and *deliver us* requests of the sixth petition of the Lord's Prayer.

Grant a good reward to all who trust in your Name,
and set our portion among them.
Then shall we never be ashamed,
  for we trust in You.
You are praised, O Lord,
  [Security] and Trust of the righteous.

And the closing doxology of the Lord's Prayer has similarities with the eighteenth benediction.

> O our King, may Your Name be
> praised and exalted continually
> and forever and ever.

Conclusions

From all of the above, we may conclude that the Lord's Prayer is essentially Jewish in intention (mark of identity), content (ideational connection with Old Testament thought), shape (twice three-fold arrangement) and direction of thought (two-fold). Parallels in content and style (brief and petitionary) are observed in the tradition of Jewish prayer. The Lord's Prayer may be said to be a miniature portrait of Jewish prayer. It is more brief as with the Half-Kaddish, and more thematically inclusive as with the Amidah. It is understandable, therefore, why Hughes Oliphant Old commented: "It may be that the Lord's Prayer, which Jesus taught his disciples, is a shortened version of the Amidah."[48]

As with the 'Shema and Its Benedictions' and the Amidah which were prayed daily in the synagogue service, so we in the Christian church traditionally have included the Lord's Prayer as an integral part of the prayers of the people in corporate worship in such locations as the people's conclusion to the Invocation, after the pastor's Prayer of Intercession (or Pastoral prayer in some traditions), at baptisms, and as a part of the observance of the Lord's Supper.

Again, as with the Jewish tradition of praying the Shema twice a day and the Amidah three times daily in private prayers, so do many Christians pray the Lord's Prayer daily, and even pattern their private prayers according to the order and content of it, as does this writer. Early on, as evidenced in *The Didache*, Christians were encouraged to pray the Lord's Prayer three times a day.[49]

---

[48] Hughes Oliphant Old. *Worship: That is Reformed According to Scripture* (Atlanta: John Knox Press, 1984), 94.

[49] James A. Kleist, trans. "The Didache," in *Ancient Christian Writers* (New York: The Newman Press, 1948), 8.3 [p. 19].

Noting the Jewish Setting

As we shall demonstrate in the remaining chapters, the Lord's Prayer is a compendium of Christian belief, one of the reasons for calling it a 'canonical prayer'. Praying it in worship is one way parishioners, perhaps without realizing it, are confessing their faith. While the Lord's Prayer is not a formal creed, it functions in corporate worship in such a way as does the Shema in Jewish worship.

Additionally, whereas Jewish prayer has a *longing* and *anticipatory* aspect to it, so also the Lord's Prayer has been described as having an eschatological tone. *Thy kingdom come* in Matthew's gospel especially falls within the context of Jesus speaking at length about the kingdom. There is no doubt the Lord's Prayer has an urgent eschatological tone and intent. However, to limit our interpretation to that aspect is a mistake. *On earth as it is in heaven, daily bread,* and *lead us not into temptation* are very now oriented. We must be reminded that our Lord spoke often with double meaning language, as the Gospel of John's content so thoroughly illustrates. For example, on many occasions Jesus spoke of the heavenly in terms of the earthly. With respect to the *kingdom* in particular, he made it clear that it is not only a *future realm* (e.g. Mt. 13:36-43, Lk. 13:28-29), but also a *present reality* (e.g. Mt. 12:28, Lk. 17:20-21).

Jewish prayer, as evidenced above, not only has future longing elements, but also present concerns. Praying the Lord's Prayer regularly in public and private worship is a way for the people of God to express their dependency upon God for all things, both for now and for later; but especially for the present.

Finally, as mentioned above, compared with many Jewish prayers, the Lord's Prayer is brief. And yet, as with the Half-Kaddish and the practice of Rabbis teaching their disciples a brief prayer which would be uniquely theirs and would serve as a mark of identity with that Rabbi, we realize the Lord's Prayer most certainly demonstrates that it is a Jewish prayer. More than that, however, with respect to its brevity, to this writer it seems that Jesus would have had in mind non-Jews who would become his followers as well. Not being familiar with Jewish prayer tradition, it would have been inappropriate to offer a prayer with more extended Jewish nuances, characteristics and content totally foreign to Gentiles. Jesus was not interested in non-Jews becoming Jews, as Peter and Paul realized and the Jerusalem Council would eventually conclude (Acts 10:34-35, 15:1-29). He wanted them to be Godly, God-worshipers, kingdom people possessing kingdom traits and dispositions, as with those given in the Beatitudes (Mt. 5:3-12). The Lord's Prayer's length makes it possible for all Christians, whether they are Gentiles or Completed Jews, to be identified with our Lord and united with one another. Community is certainly an important aspect of life generally, of Jewish history and life, of our Lord and the early church. Praying the *Lord's* Prayer in public worship is one of the ways we foster the unity of our spirits, and bind our hearts in Christian love.

Chapter Four

Addressing God

The Preface

When we communicate by letter, email, or other forms, it is customary, indeed it is the polite and appropriate thing to do, to address the correspondence by naming the person or persons receiving the message. Examples include: *Dear John, Dear Parishioners, Faithful Friends, Fellow Citizens.* It is no less appropriate when we pray to address God in a respectful manner. In the Preface of the Lord's Prayer, *Our Father who art in heaven*, we learn from Jesus a suitable address. We have all heard other fine forms of address, such as *Eternal God, Gracious God, Heavenly Father, Almighty God, Most Merciful Father,* to name a few. The address Jesus used is special, however. It serves not only as an invocation for the prayer, it teaches us to whom our prayers should be directed. It tells us something of the character of the one addressed. An indication is given of the relationships which exist between the Father and the Son and us; and, by logical deduction, we learn what are our obligations to our Father in heaven. For the sake of organization we shall discuss the above under three headings: the Title and Attributes of God, the Relationships Between God and Us, and Admonitions for Believers.

The Title and Attributes of God

The title of dignity and honor which Jesus ascribed to God was *Father*.[50] Because Jesus called God Father, it is Christ-honoring and appropriate that we should address God as Father as well. The title suggests that the God of the universe, the God of all creation is a personal divine being, not a neuter, not an it. God has a personality. He has feelings. Because the concept of God Jesus taught the disciples is

---

[50] Calvin wrote: "Father is the appellation given to him; and under this title Christ supplies us with sufficiently copius materials for confidence." *Calvin's Commentaries* Vol. XVI, 317.

personal, we understand that God is not so distant from us that he may not be reached. In other words, God is available, available as a human father could or should be to teach (Isa. 48:17, Ps. 71:17) and care for his children (Eph. 3:19, Ps. 103:13), and, when needed, to discipline them (Jer. 30:11, 1 Cor. 10:13).

Conceptualizing God as Father was a new concept in Jesus' day in near eastern religions both in number and in kind. Ancient Canaanite worship, for example, idolatry in which the Hebrews were strictly forbidden to participate, included the worship of several gods, including Asherah (or the "Lady of the Sea"), a female deity sometimes symbolized by a wooden pole with a snake coiled around it. She was also often represented as a "virgin yet pregnant goddess."[51] Moses, instructed by God, declared to the Israelites: "Hear, O Israel: The Lord our God, the Lord is one" (Deut. 6:4). When Jesus taught the disciples to pray to God as Father he was reinforcing the long-standing truth that there is only one true God and that they are to pray to that one God alone, not to any other humanly conceived gods, not to angels, not to any other highly revered or deceased personages.

This form of address was also revolutionary with regard to its imagery. Near eastern peoples thought of their gods as overlords, deities of the water, the earth, the sea, etc., who were feared and who required appeasements. To call the one true God Father suggested that divinity was personal and approachable. To put it another way, since all people have only one true biological father, so the title Father affirms that there is only one true God, not a whole cast of them, as in Greek, Roman, or any other ancient or modern system of religion, and that that one God is a caring, personal being, who loves and may be loved. William Barclay commented: "It is not that [God as Father] removes the might, majesty and power of God. It is not that it makes God any the less God; but it makes that might, and majesty, and power, approachable for us."[52] So we see that the title *Father* conveys both the singularity and affection of God.

---

[51] S. Madeleine Miller and J. Lane Miller. *Harper Bible Dictionary* (New York: Harper and Row, Publishers, 1973), 46.

[52] Barclay, *The Gospel of Matthew* Vol. 1, 202-203.

Addressing God

The address Jesus taught conveys more than this, however. *Father in heaven* tells us more about God. If God were only addressed as Father, then there could be the tendency for people to want to think of God only as a caring God who will do whatever we desire of him. People would get the impression that Judaism and Christianity are easy-going, comfortable religions. *Father in heaven* tells us not only that God is loving, he is also holy. Whereas *Father* tells us that God is approachable, *in heaven* conveys his otherness, his separateness, his dis-tinctiveness. That God the Father is in heaven suggests he is ruler, he is the head and sovereign of all because heaven is where we conceptual-ize God as being on his seat of authority, his throne, his place of honor. That place of honor and dignity and splendor are God's alone. We are not on the throne. Only God is on the throne of honor. Heaven is where God is truly manifested in glory (Ps. 103:19), and therefore, *in heaven* focuses on the holiness and the power of God.

It is noteworthy to mention that the term translated *heaven* actually exists in the plural *(ouranois)*: Our Father in the *heavens*. In the biblical conception of things, the sky was considered the first heaven. Space was thought of as the second heaven. Above space was the third heaven, the abode of God (see e.g. Gen. 1:1, Psalm 19:1, 2 Cor. 12:2). The comprehensiveness of this term, therefore, amplifies the concept of the greatness of God, his sovereignty over all creation.

Our Father in heaven is a unique conceptualization of God, only one of a kind in the world's religions; it is different from all the rest; and, therefore, that is one reason why we believe the Judeo-Christian scriptural rendering of the title and attributes of God is the only understanding God intended for humanity to have of himself. God is not only to be honored and respected with a holy fear, but he is also to be loved. God is both Holy and helpful, great and good, majestic and merciful. The term *Father* stresses the nearness of God. The term *heaven* stresses the transcendence of God. *Father in heaven* reveals God's beneficence and his magnificence. We may have access to God, and we should adore our heavenly Father.

Relationships Between God and Us

The Preface also suggests the relationships between God and us. The term Father in Jesus' spoken language of Aramaic is the word *Abba*. Geoffrey Wainwright said of the use of this term: "It was the word used from child to parent, from disciple to rabbi; it combines intimacy and respect, familiarity and esteem, affection and reverence."[53] *Abba* was not in any way a formal address, but rather a term expressing an intimate relationship. Both the psalmist and the writer of Hebrews wrote of this relationship: "You are my Son; today I have become your father" (Ps. 2:7; Heb. 1:5). To Jesus God was both Father and God, ever near and ever to be held in reverence. Jesus knew God as his Father and taught the disciples to call God Father. Indeed, he came to make it possible for people to come to know God as *our* Father. Jesus, in the intercessory prayer recorded in the Gospel of John, prayed:

> Father, the time has come. Glorify your Son, that your Son may glorify You. For you granted him authority over all people that he might give eternal life to all those you have given him. Now this is eternal life: that they may know you, the only true God, and Jesus Christ, whom you have sent (Jn. 17:1-3).

Jesus came to help us come to know the Father through himself. We understand, therefore, that God the Father is to be known as our heavenly parent, that we can have a personal relationship with God through Jesus.

What is that which enables us to call God our Father? It is faith. Paul explained: "You are all sons of God through faith in Christ Jesus" (Gal. 3:26). We may ask in what ways may God be considered our Father. God is our Father by his act of creation.[54] Malachi 2:10 asks:

---

[53] Geoffrey Wainwright. Doxology: *The Praise of God in Worship, Doctrine and Life. A Systematic Theology* (New York: Oxford University Press, 1980), 22.

[54] A word of explanation is appropriate regarding this statement. The scriptures say Jesus in his pre-human state was the person of the God-head who did the creating (Col. 1:16), and the Holy Spirit accomplished the ordering of it (Gen. 1:2). However, generally the Christian church has referred to the Father as creator, the "maker of heaven and earth" as the Apostles' Creed renders it, in the sense that he was the planner and supervisor. God (*Elohim*, a plural noun in Gen. 1:1) in all his fullness created the heavens and the earth.

Addressing God

"Have we not all one Father? Did not one God create us?" In a sermon to the Athenians, the Apostle Paul declared: "'For in him we live and move and have our being.' As some of your own poets have said, 'We are his offspring'" (Acts 17:28). All humanity has a common parentage. God is our Father by *creation*.

God is the believer's Father by *election*. Paul explained: "For he chose us in [Christ] before the creation of the world to be holy and blameless in his sight" (Eph. 1:4). Believers in Christ are God's chosen people (Jn. 15:19, Col. 3:12, 1 Pet. 1:1, 5:13). Those whom God predestined, he called (Rom. 8:30). Those who respond to God's call are the chosen of God and he is their heavenly Father.

God is the believer's Father also by *adoption*. Paul remarked: "In love he predestined us to be adopted as his sons through Jesus Christ, in accordance with his pleasure and will...In him we have redemption" (Eph. 1:5-7). The biblical metaphor for the spiritual state of grace and relationship between God and the believer (any believer, male or female, young or old) is that of an adopted son, as it was understood in Israelite culture. Who was the natural Son? Jesus, who has been called the first born among many (Rom. 8:29, Col. 1:15 & 18). Who are all the brothers? Jesus was the only begotten Son of the Father. All believers become the Father's adopted sons and daughters. They become adopted brothers and sisters of Jesus, and are co-heirs with Jesus of all the inheritance God has to bestow upon his faithful children. Paul explained:

> ...those who are led by the Spirit of God are sons of God. For you did not receive a spirit that makes you a slave again to fear, but you received the Spirit of sonship. And by him we cry, 'Abba, Father.' The Spirit testifies with our spirit that we are God's children. Now if we are children then we are heirs—heirs of God and co-heirs with Christ...(Rom. 8:14-17; see also Gal. 4:4-7).

We may call God our *Father* because he *created* us, *called* us, and *adopted* us into his family through faith in Jesus. We are to think of ourselves as related to God as his adopted children, and as brothers and sisters of Jesus. Because we have a common creator-parent, and because we are a part of a family of faith, it is appropriate to address God not as my Father, but *Our* Father. Additionally, to say *Our Father* helps us keep a proper perspective in our prayers. It reduces the significance of self, and elevates the position of God and the collective nature and responsibility of believers.

We pray in the name of Jesus, or through Jesus Christ, because he is the one who taught his disciples how to pray. He is the one through whom we gain access to God and adoption into God's family. To repeat, we call God *Father* because Jesus, God incarnate, addressed God in that fashion. The authority and example for calling God *Father*, therefore, comes from God himself!

Admonitions for Believers

Having discussed the preface of the Lord's Prayer from the standpoints of the title and attributes of God, and the relationships between God and us, we may now offer several admonitions as logical outcomes of the above considerations.

Because *Our Father in heaven* is our creator, we, his children, are obliged, indeed, we want to honor God by addressing him respectfully in prayer. By calling on God in prayer, we honor God. William Barclay commented:

> We must never use the word Father in regard to God cheaply, easily, and sentimentally. God is not an easy-going parent who tolerantly shuts his eyes to all sins and faults and mistakes. This God, whom we can call Father, is the God whom we must still approach with reverence and adoration, and awe and wonder. God is our Father in heaven, and in God there is love and holiness combined.[55]

Our Father is our heavenly provider. We should trust and rely upon him for all our needs, consult him regarding all our desires, and seek his will for our lives. We should humble ourselves before him and submit

---

[55] Barclay, *The Gospel of Matthew* Vol. 1, 204.

to his direction. Jesus submitted to the Father's will (Heb. 5:7). So should we. Because *Our Father in heaven* is not only majestic but merciful, we can and we should approach God to seek forgiveness for our sins, which he freely provides to those who are truly repentant and have committed their lives to Christ, our redeemer. Paul said: "Since we are God's offspring...then repent." (Acts 17:29-30). Because God the Father is our heavenly parent, we should be aware that he may discipline us as needed. This should move us to want to conduct our lives according to his standards of behavior, acting as thankful and respectful children. Jesus knew God as Father, and he entered our arena to enable us to know God as Father as well. The preface of the Lord's Prayer, therefore, serves as a reminder of the call of God extended to all the world. God desires to be known and loved. The call is extended through the church to love the Lord our God (Deut. 6:5). The preface establishes God the Father in heaven as the One to whom all prayer should be addressed.

Chapter Five

Hallowing God's Name

Petition One

In the two previous chapters we offered an introduction to the Lord's Prayer and considered the meanings of the preface: *Our Father in heaven*. Here we focus on the first of the six petitions of the prayer: *Hallowed be thy name* or, as we might render it, *May your name be hallowed*. The first three petitions of the prayer deal with divine matters: God's name, God's kingdom, and God's will. The second group of three petitions is concerned with human needs: daily necessities, forgiveness, and protection against evil. In the first petition we encounter two important terms: *Hallowed* and *Name*. We shall interpret them in order, and then relate the petition to our everyday lives. *Our Father in heaven, may your name be hallowed.*

Defining Hallow

Hallow is a term not in common usage. The only other related word with which most people are familiar is *Halloween*. Originally the observance we now call Halloween was called All Hallows Eve. It was so called because October 31 was the night before All Saints, a holy day in some traditions set aside to honor the sacred memory of departed believers. *Hallowed* is a form of the New Testament Greek verb to *hallow (hagiazesthai)*, meaning to treat a person or a thing as holy *(hagios)*. The literal meaning of the term *holy* is different, separate, and, therefore, special. Something which is holy, something which is hallowed, is something which is different from other things. A person who is holy, hallowed, is separate, special from other people. The Bible is the *Holy* Bible because it is special, separate, sacred, different from other collections of writings.

The petition, *Hallowed be thy name*, means therefore: May God's name be treated differently from all other names; May God's name be given special treatment and a position which is absolutely unique and honorable.[56] Hallowing God's name means to *set it apart* from common usage, to keep it holy, to magnify the name of the Lord.[57] Calvin rendered the petition: "May thy name be sanctified... To sanctify the name of God means nothing else, than to give unto the Lord the glory due unto his name, so that [people] may never think or speak of [God] but with the deepest veneration... The substance of this petition is, that the glory of God may shine in the world, and may be duly acknowledged by [all]."[58]

The Significance of the Name of God

Next we consider the significance of the *name* of God. We shall cite a few words in the Bible used as names for God, and then relate further what is the meaning of names in the ancient Hebrew culture.

Jesus said: "This, then, is how you should pray: Our Father in heaven, hallowed be your name." Jesus called God *Father*. We have spoken extensively about this title, that it is a term which established the fact that God is a personal being; he is approachable; he cares about us. Father in *heaven* signifies also his otherness, his holiness. Because Jesus called God Father, so may we; but where did the word *God* come from? God in English is the equivalent of the Old Testament Hebrew term *El*, a term common in ancient near eastern societies, which literally means, the *all-powerful one*. There are a variety of names for God used by the Hebrews as recorded in the Old Testament such as *Elohim* (Gen. 1:1), the plural form of El. It may indicate God exists as a plural being. God is also called *El-Shaddai* (Gen. 17:1) which means *God almighty*, and *El-Olam* (Gen. 21:33), meaning *Eternal God*. Jesus was called *Emmanuel* which means *God with us*, indicating that *Jesus* was God in human form. *Jesus* therefore, may be thought of as a *name* for God. Tertullian remarked: "The Son is now the Father's new name."[59]

---

[56] Barclay, *The Gospel of Matthew* Vol. 1, 205.

[57] Watson, 51.

[58] *Calvin's Commentaries* Vol. XVI, 318.

[59] Tertullian. "On Prayer," *Ante-Nicene Fathers* Vol. 3, 662.

In the Old Testament we find a very important name for God. We discover it, for example, in Exodus 3:14. The context of the citation is God's calling Moses to be the deliverer of the Israelites. Moses said to God:

> Suppose I go to the Israelites and say to them, "The God of your Fathers has sent me to you," and they ask me, "what is his name?" Then what shall I tell them? God said to Moses, "I AM WHO I AM." This is what you are to say to the Israelites: "I AM has sent me to you"...This is my name forever, the name by which I am to be remembered from generation to generation" (Ex. 3:13-15).

I AM is also sometimes rendered *LORD*. While one term, *adonai*, in scripture is rendered Lord, meaning *master, LORD* in the sense of *I AM* is translated from the Hebrew *Yahweh*; in English, *Jehovah*. Literally *Yahweh, I AM,* and *Jehovah* mean the *eternal self-existent one*. *El* (God), therefore, is the *eternal present-one*.

The name *Yahweh* was so hallowed by the Hebrews, considered by them sacred, that it was sparingly spoken for many years during their history. Yahweh/Jehovah is the most prominent name for God in the Bible. The term *hallelujah* was used so as not to speak fully the holy name of God. *Hallelu* means praise. *Yah*, is an abbreviation of Yahweh. *Halleluyah* means, therefore, *praise Yahweh*, praise the eternal present one, *praise the Lord!*

In the ancient near east, a name was not simply a word by which a person was identified. In our day a name is a convenient label by which to differentiate one person or thing from another. In biblical times a name meant the nature, the character and the personality of the one addressed. For example Jacob, which means *one whom God protects*, one who literally *struggled* with a divine being, was renamed *Israel*, which means *he struggles with God*. The nation named for Jacob (Israel), has been struggling ever since. The name refers to the character of the one so identified. To speak *God's* name, therefore, is to refer to God's character. God's name is God essence. *God's self* is concentrated in his *name*: Yahweh, Jehovah, Elohim, El-Shaddai, El-Olam, etc. *Jesus,* which means *one who saves*, was so named because he would be the *Savior* of many. He was characterized as *Emmanuel*, because he was God in human form, *El* with us. When Christians pray *Hallowed be thy name*, therefore, it means: Enable us to give to you, O God, the special place in our lives which your nature and character demand.[60] In other words, we are to have reverence for God's name, to respect and use God's name as a term of adoration when we address God or speak about *Our Father in heaven*. Luther put it this way: "He should receive from us the glory that is due Him, and His name should be held in high esteem throughout the world."[61] When we speak of God it should mean something significant.

We should add that each one of the first three petitions, *hallowed be thy name, thy kingdom come,* and t*hy will be done,* is prayed that it be accomplished *on earth as it is in heaven*. As God's rule is firm in heaven, we pray people on earth will accept God's rule in their lives. As God's will is established in heaven, we pray that his will may be carried out on earth generally, and in people's individual lives specifically. As God's name, his form of address and his character are glorified in heaven, we pray his name may be spoken and honored in all the earth. Shortly, we shall discuss *how* we hallow God's name. First, however, we must consider what too often occurs on earth, the antithesis of hallowing God's name.

The Antithesis of Hallowing God's Name

Since to hallow God's name means to venerate the name of the Lord, to regard the name and character of God with the deepest respect, we realize the opposite of veneration is *profanation*. To profane the name of God is to use the name of God disrespectfully. What comes to mind, of course, is the third commandment. Third on the summary of God's standards for human behavior is: "Thou shalt not take the name of the LORD thy God in vain" (Ex. 20:7 KJV). The NIV renders it: "You shall not misuse the name of the LORD your God..." The *Jerusalem*

---

[60] Barclay, *The Gospel of Matthew* Vol. 1, 206.
[61] *Luther's Works* Vol. 2, III, XX, 41.

Bible correctly reads: "You shall not utter the name of Yahweh your God to misuse it..."

The opposite of hallowing God's name, therefore, would include any usage of God's name which would detract from God's true character, any usage which would not convey the specialness and uniqueness of God. Frivolous usage of God's name in common discourse, casual reference to the name of God in everyday speech without regard for what one is saying, is misusing the name of God. How many times do we hear people thoughtlessly say "Oh God" this, "Oh God" that, or "Oh my God;" God used as a minced-oath, an exclamation? Why is it wrong to say "Oh God" as a casual expression? Because God's name is to be hallowed, set apart from the everyday, held in high esteem. The second half of Ex 20:7 says in the NIV: "for the LORD will not hold anyone guiltless who misuses his name." Leviticus 24:10-16 records the account of the son of an Israelite mother and an Egyptian father. The young man *blasphemed*, that is, *insulted* the name of God with a curse. He was taken outside the camp and stoned to death by the entire assembly, as directed by God through Moses. If the Mosaic regulation were in effect in our society, imagine how many people would be executed for misusing God's name!

Again, why is honoring God's name so important? Because God's name signifies his character. Misusing his name *misrepresents* God. God's majesty is violated; his character is cheapened. God is not known for who he really is and what he is supposed to mean in peoples' lives. Calvin said nothing could be more unworthy of us than to obscure the glory of God by the misuse of his name.[62] Using God's name meaninglessly and thoughtlessly serves to ruin the name and reputation of God in general society. Matthew Henry wrote in *The Pleasantness of a Religious Life*: "Compare the hellish pleasure which some take in profaning the name of God, and the heavenly pleasure which others have in glorifying it, and tell me which is preferable."[63]

---

[62] John T. McNeill, ed. *Calvin: Institutes of the Christian Religion* Vol. 2, III, XX, 41.

[63] Matthew Henry. *The Pleasantness of a Religious Life* (Morgan, Pennsylvania: Soli Deo Gloria Publications, 1996), 59.

Needless to say, to use *Jesus'* name as an exclamation is a misuse of God's name as well, as he was God incarnate. To do so is a violation of the third commandment.

Another example of misusing God's name was given by Calvin. His commentary focused on citing God's name in the swearing or making of oaths or vows. If someone, for example, swore in the name of God that something was true when it was not true, that would be perjury, abusing the name of God by citing it when telling a lie. Not only so, Calvin said that God's name is taken in vain when it is "lightly and disrespectfully adduced in proof of frivolous and trifling matters."[64] For example, a child coming home late from school may say to his or her mother: "Mom, I had to stay after school to help the teacher, honest to God." That is a frivolous, self-serving, and meaningless usage of God's name. Calvin warned his readers to be very cautious and sparing in making oaths in the name of God. Christians are to do so only when it means something.[65]

When an elected official swears in the name of God to do his or her best in office, and then disregards God's advice from the scriptures on how to govern and make decisions, what to promote and what not to support, then that individual is guilty of misrepresenting the name of God. It would be better not to invoke the name of God in such instances. Interestingly enough the Jewish Bible rendering of Ex. 20:7 reads: "You shall not swear falsely by the name of the LORD your God; for the LORD will not clear one who swears falsely by His name."[66] Calvin was right on target. From the above we may say with assurance, therefore, that God's name can be dishonored in words and with deeds, in speech and in actions which are the antithesis of the *proper* representation of the character of God. "As it brings shame and disgrace on an

---

[64] John Calvin. "Commentaries on the Four Last Books of Moses Arranged in the Form of a Harmony" Volume Second. *Calvin's Commentaries* Vol. II (Grand Rapids: Baker Book House, 1993), 409.

[65] Ibid., 416.

[66] *TANAKH. The Holy Scriptures.* The New JPS Translation According to the Traditional Hebrew Text (Philadelphia: The Jewish Publication Society, 1985), 115; see also Matthew 5:33-37.

earthly father when a child goes bad in speech and conduct, so also do we dishonor God when we teach, speak, or live otherwise than as godly children."[67]

One final word on this subject which I will simply mention is also a violation of God's name and reputation; namely, to worship other than the one true God, which is idolatry. To ascribe glory to an object, another person, or to a hypothetical deity as if it were the Supreme Being, is the ultimate misrepresentation of El, Yahweh, the eternal existent-one.

Hallowing the Name of God

Finally, from an understanding of the first petition of the Lord's Prayer, we may make application to our lives. How do we hallow the name of God? In the largest sense, to hallow God's name means to honor God in our speech and in our conduct. Actually speaking God's name should be done so when specifically speaking to God or speaking meaningfully about God. Why? Because when we speak the name of God we are making God known.[68] John Wesley preached:

> In praying that God, or his name, may be hallowed or glorified, we pray that he may be known, such as he is, by all that are capable thereof, by all intelligent beings, and with affections suitable to that knowledge; that he may be duly honored, and feared, and loved, by all in heaven above and in the earth beneath; by all angels and men, whom for that end he has made capable of knowing and loving him to eternity.[69]

Therefore, we hallow God's name as we speak of him with respect and as we live respectable lives. As Luther said, may "his name never

---

[67] F. Samuel Janzow. *Luther's Large Catechism*, 84-85.

[68] Augustine. "Our Lord's Sermon on the Mount." *Nicene and Post-Nicene Fathers* Vol. 6, Philip Schaff, ed. (Peabody, Mass: Hendrickson Publishers, 1994), 40.

[69] John Wesley, 335.

be put to shame by us either in teaching or in life."[70] We need to control our tongues and guard our lives. We hallow God's name by letting our light so shine before others, that they may see our good works and hear our proper speech, and glorify our Father in heaven (Mt. 5:16). Thomas Watson explained that we hallow God's name by having a high appreciation and esteem for him, and set him highest in our thoughts; when we truly believe him and give our lives to him, putting him first in our lives; when we obey his Word; when we attend worship, thus honoring his day; when we honor Christ; when we stand up for God's truths; and when we make as many converts as possible.[71] David Jeremiah adds we hallow God's name by recognizing regularly his presence in our lives.[72]

In short, Christians are God's advertisements. Others may be more likely to consider commitment to God if they see and hear faithful representatives speaking and acting as God intends. We are admonished to be faithful in "the advancement of his Glory,"[73] not our own. *May your name be hallowed* ultimately is a petition that God may be known, loved, worshiped, held in high esteem by people everywhere on planet earth. Let us kneel our hearts and indeed our whole selves before the Father from whom the entire company in heaven and on earth derives its name (Eph. 3:15).

> "O Lord, our Lord, how majestic is your name in all the earth!"(Psalm 8:9). "[May your name] be made visible through us, in the midst of us, by the severity and the serenity of our lives, of our customs, and of our ethics. We pray so that we may receive the power to show this great joy and this great

---

[70] Martin Luther. "Ten Sermons on the Catechism, 1528," *Luther's Works* Vol. 51, John W. Doberstein, ed. & trans., & Helmut T. Lehmann, ed. (Philadelphia: Fortress Press, 1959), 173.

[71] Watson, 39-44.

[72] David Jeremiah, 95.

[73] *Calvin's Commentaries* Vol. XVI, 318.

peace of which we so often speak. May this joy and this peace be noticeable. We pray in order that the Christian arrogance and ignorance and unbelief with which we daily dishonor [you] may be a bit arrested, a little suppressed."[74] Our Father in heaven, hallowed be thy name. We pray through Jesus Christ our Lord. Amen.

---

[74] Karl Barth. *Prayer* sec. ed. (Philadelphia: The Westminster Press, 1985), 56.

Chapter Six

Entering the Kingdom of God

Petition Two, Part One

For a nation which decided from its inception that it would not be governed by a monarchy, there has been in our history a great interest in royalty. I'm told that on a stone marker laid in Germantown, Pennsylvania during the Revolutionary War, there is an inscription which says: "We will serve no sovereign." And yet newspapers and magazines in this country, as well as in Great Britain, keep up with the romance, if you will, of the goings on with the Royal family in England. In our own nation some have likened the era of the Presidency of John F. Kennedy to Camelot. A well-known jazz pianist has been referred to as Duke. Elvis is called the King of Rock 'n Roll. And boxing's Muhammed Ali said of himself: "I am the king!"

In biblical times a king who was returning from a battle would ride into his home city on horseback greeted by throngs of people who waved palm branches and laid some on the road. When the word was out that Jesus, who had gained quite a reputation for teaching and healing, was coming to Jerusalem, many followers decided they would welcome him in the way kings were welcomed. However, Jesus did not enter Jerusalem on horseback. He came in on a donkey, a humble beast of burden. Thus was sent a message that he came in humility and in peace, not as a military conqueror. If anyone looked to him as king of the Jews, he communicated by the way he entered the city that the kind of kingship he offered was not the usual kind people expected or even desired of a ruler of an earthly kingdom. After his arrest he was interrogated by Pilate, the Roman Governor, who asked him: "Are you the king of the Jews?" Jesus said: "My kingdom is not of this world...my kingdom is from another place...You are right in saying I am a king. In fact, for this reason I was born and for this I came into the world...." (from Jn 18:33, 36-37).

A king has a kingdom, and Jesus' kingdom is called the *kingdom of*

God. During his days of ministry Jesus spoke much about the kingdom of God. When he taught the disciples how to pray he included the petition: *Thy kingdom come,* or, as we may render it, *May your kingdom come.* We're going to spend some time understanding what *kingdom* means and how it does or can *come.* Then we shall explore more fully how persons *enter* the kingdom of God.

Defining Kingdom

One of the ways God is portrayed in scripture is as a king. For example, Psalm 47:7-8 says: "For God is the King of all the earth; sing to him a psalm of praise. God reigns over the nations; God is seated on his holy throne." God is pictured as the high and lofty One (Isa. 57:15), a great and glorious sovereign (Ps. 95:3, Ps. 24:10). If God is a king then he must have a kingdom. From the Psalm 47 citation we may discern his kingdom is *two dimensional*; that there is an *earthly* aspect to the kingdom ("all the earth" and "over the nations"); and that there is a *heavenly* component as well ("God is seated on his holy throne"). There is a *here* zone, if you will, and a *there* zone. So we may say there is the matter of *location* of the kingdom of God with which we may be concerned. Obviously God rules there (in heaven). In the Lord's Prayer we petition God that he rule on earth as well.

The term *kingdom (basileia)* denotes sovereignty or dominion. It is used as a figure of speech referring to a territory or people whom a king rules.[75] The *kingdom of God*, therefore, is the sphere of God's rule or the sphere where God's rule is acknowledged. Wherever God rules, here or there, is the kingdom of God.

Other characteristics of the kingdom of God with which we may be concerned include *time, location* and *kind.* Matthew records John the Baptist's preaching in the Desert of Judea saying: "Repent, for the kingdom of heaven is near" (3:1-2). After John was imprisoned Jesus began preaching the same message (4:17). What did John and Jesus mean by the *nearness* of the kingdom? That it would soon take place or that it

---

[75] W. E. Vine. *An Expository Dictionary of New Testament Words* (Nashville: Thomas Nelson, Publishers, 1952), 624.

was close at hand and could be touched or reached? Probably both. *Near* is explained most appropriately, however, by another expression of Jesus. Luke 17:20-21 records: "Once, having been asked by the Pharisees when the kingdom of God would come, Jesus replied, 'The kingdom of God does not come with careful observation, nor will people say, 'Here it is,' or 'There it is,' because the kingdom of God is within you." *Within you* could also be rendered *among you* or *in your midst*. What did Jesus mean? Our Savior described a kingdom unlike the world has ever known. Rather than a kingdom with outward ceremony and political organization, his kingdom is a kingdom of the spirit. He said: "My kingdom is not of this world" (Jn. 18:36). The Apostle Paul put it this way: "The kingdom of God is not a matter of eating and drinking, but of righteousness, peace and joy in the Holy Spirit" (Rom. 14:17).

The sayings of Jesus also make it clear that the kingdom of God is a particular *kind* of kingdom and that it exists or can exist in the *present*. It is a *present reality*, something which takes place within people as well among them. When we pray the petition in the Lord's Prayer, however, praying *Thy kingdom come*, or *May your kingdom come*, we understand the petition has a *future* element to it as well. Indeed, Jesus also spoke of the kingdom in the future tense. From Luke 13:29 we read Jesus' teaching that in the future "people will come from east and west and north and south, and will take their places at the feast in the kingdom of God." This sounds a lot like the description of the gathering of the elect at the second coming of Christ as given in Matthew 24:29-31.

> Immediately after the distress of those days...the sign of the Son of Man will appear in the sky, and all the nations of the earth will mourn. They will see the Son of Man coming on the clouds of the sky, with power and great glory. And he will send his angels with a loud trumpet call, and they will gather his elect from the four winds, from one end of the heavens to the other.

The future aspect of the kingdom, the ultimate completion of it, is what those who cite the Jewish setting of the Lord's Prayer often emphasize, as mentioned in Chapter Three. However, the kingdom of God is not only a *future* realm, it also a *present* reality (near, within you, among you, in your midst). The kingdom of God exists when and where the rule of God takes place *within* the lives of individuals in the *present*, and when and where the rule of God is and shall forever be established in the heavenly realm (see also Lk. 13:28). The kingdom of God occurs *here* and *there*; on earth as it is in heaven. Because the kingdom of God happens in the present and in the future, we understand there is an *already* aspect to the kingdom, and a *not yet* aspect. When we pray "thy kingdom come" we are praying that the rule of God may take over in our lives and in many peoples' lives now; that people on earth in the present may submit to the dominion of God in their lives. The petition also includes the meaning that we long for the ushering in of the kingdom of God in the future, where that which is being actualized already in our lives will be fulfilled and consummated at the coming of Jesus in the end of days, when the dead in Christ will rise and those who are alive and remain will be caught up together to be with Christ forever (1 Th. 4:16-17; 1 Cor. 15:51-53). Augustine (354-430) put it this way: "Then will the blessed life in all its parts be perfected in the saints unto eternity..."[76]

Thomas Watson described the here and present reality as the *kingdom of God's grace*, whereby God's grace is extended to "the consciences of his people."[77] Watson explained: "When we pray 'thy kingdom come' we pray that the kingdom of grace may be set up in our hearts and increased."[78] He called the there and future realm of the kingdom of God the *kingdom of God's glory*. He explained that when we pray the petition:

> we pray also that the kingdom of glory may hasten, and that we may, in God's good time be translated into it. There is such an inseparable connection between these two kingdoms, grace and glory, that there is no passing into the one but by the

---

[76] Augustine, 40.

[77] Watson, 59.

[78] Ibid.

other....the kingdoms of grace and glory are so closely joined together, that we cannot go into the kingdom of glory but through the kingdom of grace. Many people aspire after the kingdom of glory, but never look after grace; but these two, which God hath joined together, may not be put asunder: The kingdom of grace leads to the kingdom of glory.[79]

Entering the Kingdom of God's Grace

Because, as Watson states, "there is such an inseparable connection between these two kingdoms, grace and glory," and "that there is no passing into the one but by the other," and, it would seem, most persons would look favorably upon the notion of being in the kingdom of God's glory in the hereafter, it behooves us to consider how the kingdom of God's grace is set up in peoples lives, which is the *prerequisite* for translation into the kingdom of God's glory.

Jesus said: "The kingdom of God does not come with your careful observation, nor will people say, 'Here it is,' or 'there it is,' because the kingdom of God is within you" (Lk. 17:20-21). The now dimension of the kingdom of God is called the kingdom of God's grace because it is by God's grace that any of us are forgiven of our sins and justified for entry into the kingdom. The Bible teaches that all people sin and fall short of God's standards for human behavior and, therefore, fall short of God's requirements for habitation in the kingdom of Glory (Rom. 3:23). Moreover, the scriptures teach that the wages, the payment for our sin is not only physical but spiritual death. Because of sin we human beings are dead spiritually, dead in our ability to discern well enough the things of God, dead in our capacities to do the right things all the time. It is only because of the mercy and unmerited favor of God (God's grace), that any of us are awakened to the things of the Spirit. Otherwise all would perish. None would gain entry into the kingdom of God's glory. This is the core of the gospel: God so loved the world that he offered his only Son that whoever believes in him will

---

[79] Ibid., 59-60

not perish, but have everlasting life with God, beginning now and leading to the rest of eternity (Jn. 3:16). How persons gain entrance into the kingdom of God's grace is by *faith* in Jesus (Rom. 3:22-28), by trusting in him, asking his spirit to enter their lives within, by permitting him to rule in their thinking, decisions, and activities. *The kingdom of God's grace comes when persons pray and invite the Spirit of Jesus Christ to take up residence in their hearts* (see Mt. 7:7-8, Jn. 1:12, 3:16, Acts 2:37-38, Rom. 10:8-13, Col. 2:6, 1 Jn. 4:15, Rev. 3:20). It is by faith in Jesus Christ that we are justified to enter (Rom. 3:20-28, Rom. 5:1-2, Eph. 2:8-9).

Thomas Watson described believers' union with Jesus Christ as being "incorporated into Christ, they are knit to him as members of the head, by the nerve and ligament of faith..."[80] Believers gain entry into the kingdom "by virtue of their coalition and union with Jesus Christ..."[81] Watson exhorted: "Let us go to God to set up this kingdom of grace in our hearts... Keep close to the word preached... It is the great engine He uses for setting up the kingdom of grace in the heart...,"[82] because faith comes through the hearing of the word of God preached (Rom. 10:17).

When people pray *thy kingdom come* they are asking, as Calvin wrote, that God "may remove all hindrances, and may bring all [people] under his dominion and may lead them to meditate on the heavenly life... This is done partly by the preaching of the Word and partly by the secret power of the Spirit."[83] "God is said to reign among [people], when they voluntarily devote and submit themselves to be governed by him..."[84] When people pray *may your kingdom come*, they pray, therefore, "that God would exert his power, both by the Word," which is preached and taught and shared, "and by the Spirit," by which God prompts and leads, and with which he imparts to the believer, "that the

---

[80] Ibid., 132.

[81] Ibid., 96.

[82] Ibid., 75.

[83] *Calvin's Commentaries* XVI, 319.

[84] Ibid., 320.

whole world may willingly submit to him."[85]

Martin Luther put it this way: "...it is our prayer that through the leading of the Holy Spirit many may come into the kingdom of grace and share salvation with us, so that together we may continue forever in the kingdom that has now begun among us."[86] Why are there not more people in the kingdom? *Unbelief* is the reason. People are too much attached to the things of this world, its temporal pleasures, and they have a very limited view or no view of heavenly things or of their own eternal destiny.[87] We persist, therefore, in the work of Jesus, doing what he called us to do: to preach the gospel, to make disciples in all the world (Mt. 28:19-20, Mk. 16:15-16, 2 Tim. 4:2-5). Calvin declared that we are called to entreat God to bring the minds and hearts of people into voluntary obedience.[88]

One of the most significant passages of scripture which explains how people enter the kingdom of God's grace is the third chapter of the Gospel of John. When the Pharisee Nicodemus came to Jesus, our Lord explained: "I tell you the truth, no one can [enter] the kingdom of God unless he is born again." Nicodemus asked: "How can a man be born when he is old?" Whereas Nicodemus was thinking in *earthly* terms, Jesus was speaking of *heavenly* things. Jesus answered: "I tell you the truth, no one can enter the kingdom of God unless he is born of water and the Spirit. Flesh gives birth to flesh, but Spirit gives birth to spirit,... you must be born again" (Jn. 3:3-7). The *birth of the spirit* is the second birth of which the scriptures speak. It is the requirement for entry into the kingdom of God's grace. That is what is meant by uniting with Christ, pledging or professing faith in Jesus, receiving Jesus Christ into one's life, being converted, being born again. All these mean the *birth of the spirit*. It is in this conversation with Nicodemus where Jesus spoke those famous words of John 3:16, after which he

---

[85] Ibid.

[86] Janzow, 86.

[87] Ibid., 87.

[88] *Institutes* Vol. 2, III, XX, 42. See also III, III, 19 and III, VI-X for more on the kingdom of God.

explained further: "whoever believes in [the Son] is not condemned, but whoever does not believe stands condemned already because he has not believed in the name of God's one and only Son" (Jn. 3:18). Unbelief is what hinders people from entry into the kingdom. When we pray *thy kingdom come* we not only ask of God that many people all over the earth may invite the rule of Christ into their lives as it is in heaven; but also "we pray that the kingdom of grace may come into our hearts."[89] John Wesley preached: "this kingdom comes to a particular person when he repents and believes the gospel when [he comes] to know Jesus Christ...This is...the kingdom of God begun below, set up in the believer's heart."[90] Unless the kingdom comes to dwell within us we are out of fellowship with God, our spirits are not alive to the things of God, and we are not qualified for the kingdom of God's glory. Are you qualified? Have you entered the kingdom of God's grace? Have you invited the Spirit of Jesus Christ into your life?

We need to make one further point regarding the word *come* in the petition (*eltheto* [become] *he basileai sou*). The verb most literally means *come into being*.[91] Its usage, therefore, suggests: "let your kingdom come into being."[92] "Let it happen, let it appear, let it arise, let it take place." The verb usage makes it practically impossible to interpret the petition as a reference to any gradual process or evolution leading ultimately to a perfect society on earth. Rather, the language implies a *sudden change* as in a moment, as in the twinkling of any eye, that quickly. The message is clear. When Jesus taught the disciples to pray to the Father "let your kingdom come," he was referring in part to the instantaneous change in believers' lives the moment they genuinely trust in Jesus Christ as Savior of their souls and the Lord of their living. At such a moment, whether known and remembered or not, a person's spirit is birthed, a life has entered the kingdom of God's grace.

---

[89] Watson, 62.

[90] John Wesley, 336.

[91] Vine, 625.

[92] Barclay, *The Gospel of Matthew* Vol. 1, 210.

Has the kingdom of God's grace been set up in your heart? Are you born of the spirit? Have you surrendered your life to Jesus Christ as Savior and Lord? The kingdom of God comes into being in our lives when we make that pledge of faith. All who have yet to take that step of faith are here encouraged to consider doing so, because that's the prerequisite for a truly happy and purposeful life now; and it is the requirement for our being welcomed into the kingdom of God's glory in the hereafter.

Chapter Seven

Increasing in the Kingdom of God

Petition Two, Part Two

There's an old chorus which says:

> *This world is not my home,*
> *I'm just a passing through,*
> *My treasures are laid up*
> *Somewhere beyond the blue,*
> *The angels beckon me*
> *From heaven's open door,*
> *And I can't feel at home*
> *In this world any more.*

This world is not my home, I'm just passing through. For many years, as far back as teenage days, I can remember making the remark to one person or another, that truly I felt and believed (and still I feel and believe) that this world is not my home, that I'm passing through this life on route to another and permanent home. Oh, certain places where we've lived became more like home to us than others. However, being anywhere now is fine because anywhere is somewhere in this journey toward our ultimate destination, our eternal residence. How we journey, how we spend our passing, what should take place in believers' lives between the moment they enter the kingdom of God's grace and the moment they are translated into the kingdom of God's glory, should be of concern to us as Christians, that we may be effective witnesses for Christ now and be more fit for our home above. That is one of the concerns of the second petition of the Lord's Prayer.

UNITED IN PRAYER

How our time is spent in the kingdom of God's grace has significance for the success of Christ' work in the here and now, as well as for our passage to and ultimate reception in the kingdom of God's glory. "Faith without deeds is dead" (Jas. 2:26), it is lifeless, useless. Faith which does not have good works as a part of its nature and expression is non-faith. When persons enter the kingdom of God's grace, they must be and do something of significance in the kingdom. The rule of God must *take shape* in persons' lives. Believers must accept the *responsibilities* of membership in the kingdom. *Manifestation* serves as an *indication*, a *validation*, and a means of *preservation* of one's profession of faith. Inner spiritual growth and outer expression are expected, and are the means by which the status of believers with God is maintained, so that they shall stay on track and receive a rich welcome in the kingdom of God's glory. Persons who pledge faith in Christ, are intended to grow in Christ. This is what is called *sanctification*, the process of *progressive transformation into Christlikeness*. Paul explained that during this life Christians "are being transformed into his likeness with ever-increasing glory, which comes from the Lord, who is the Spirit" (2 Cor. 3:18). So we need to think about what is involved in the spiritual growth process because it is the means by which we successfully pass through this world on route to the kingdom of God's glory. This process includes both tending to inward spiritual character and to outward matters of Christian expression and service. Both serve to point believers in the right direction, keep thoughts and behavior on the right track, and ensure that they shall reach "the goal to win the prize for which God has called [us] heavenward in Christ Jesus" (Phil. 3:14). Thomas Watson wrote: "When we pray 'Thy kingdom come,' we pray that the kingdom of grace may be set up in our hearts and increased."[93]

We shall divide our consideration into three categories: the *expectation* of God that Christians increase; the *methodology* of increasing; and the *values* or benefits of increasing in the kingdom.

---

[93] Watson, 59.

The Expectation that Christians Increase

The Bible teaches us that all who have named the name of Jesus Christ, all who have committed their lives to Christ by profession of faith, are to grow as Christians. It is intended that believers make progress in the Lord. God expects his people to develop, to *mature*, so that their relationship and their service to God may steadily increase. Paul exhorted the Colossians to "live a life worthy of the Lord and may please him in every way; bearing fruit in every good work, growing in the knowledge of God, being strengthened with all power according to his glorious might so that you may have great endurance and patience, and joyfully giving thanks to the Father, who has qualified you to share in the inheritance of the saints in the kingdom of light" (1:10-12). God expects believers to grow in knowledge, to grow by bearing fruit, by working for him. Paul encouraged: "So then, just as you received Christ Jesus as Lord, continue to live in him, rooted and built up in him, strengthened in the faith as you were taught, and overflowing with thankfulness" (Col. 2:6-7). In the introduction to his first letter to the Thessalonians Paul wrote: "We ought always to thank God for you, brothers, and rightly so, because your faith is growing more and more, and the love every one of you has for each other is increasing" (1:3). To the Philippians Paul declared: "...I desire to depart and be with Christ... but it is necessary for you that I remain... I will continue with all of you for your progress and joy in the faith" (1:23-25).

Christians are called to *mature*. In Ephesians 4 we read Paul's explanation of the various types of leaders (pastors, teachers, evangelists) God has raised up for the edification of the church. It is intended that these leaders help "prepare God's people for works of service, so that the body of Christ may be built up until we all reach unity in the faith and in the knowledge of the Son of God and become mature..." (4:13; see also Col. 4:12, Heb. 5:14). Hebrews 6:1 says: "...let us leave the elementary teaching about Christ and go on to maturity..."

Those who profess faith in Christ are intended to increase in mirroring the character of Christ in their lives. It is expected that a progressive transformation into Christlikeness take place (2 Cor. 3:18), as illustrated by Jesus in his Parable of the Yeast (Mt. 13:33). Jesus said: "The kingdom of heaven is like yeast that a woman took and mixed into a large amount of flour until it worked all through the dough." Leaven was a piece of highly fermented dough left over from a previous baking and inserted in meal in the kneading trough in order for the next bread to rise. In the scriptures leaven is almost always used as a picture for evil influence. The Israelites connected fermentation with putrefaction, the leaven standing for that which is evil (see Mt. 16:6, 1 Cor. 5:6-8, Gal. 5:9).[94] For the Passover Feast, therefore, no leaven was to be used in preparing the bread of remembrance. However, in the parable, Jesus was saying that whereas leaven transforms the character of that which is to be baked, so also the kingdom of God which is in us (Jn. 14:17) is expected to transform increasingly believers' minds and behavior.

God expects the redeemed to validate, develop and express their salvation through good works. Three important citations make the point. Paul wrote to the Philippians: "...my dear friends... continue to work out your salvation with fear and trembling, for it is God who works in you to will and to act according to his good purpose" (Phil. 2:12-13). James explained: "Faith, by itself, if it is not accompanied by action, is dead" (Jas. 2:17). Peter in his first letter encouraged his readers to make every effort to increase their faith with the cultivation of Godly character traits, such as goodness, knowledge, self-control, perseverance, piety, kindness and love. He wrote: "For if you possess these qualities in increasing measure, they will keep you from being ineffective and unproductive..." and will contribute to making "your calling and election sure. For if you do these things, you will never fall, and you will receive a rich welcome into the eternal kingdom of our Lord and Savior Jesus Christ" (2 Pet. 1:5-11). It is expected that Christians work at increasing in faith, growing in character, pressing on to maturity, expressing their commitment, validating their profession, firming up their status with God.

It is also the plan of God that together believers work to increase the number of disciples of Jesus Christ. The Great Commission of Jesus makes this perfectly clear. As believers go into all the world they are

---

[94] William Barclay, *The Gospel of Matthew* Vol. 2, 79.

called to make disciples, baptize them, and teach them (Mt. 28:19-20, Mk. 16:15). That is the ministry of the Church. It is expected that Christians assume the responsibility for increasing the kingdom of God's grace *numerically*. Jesus' parable of the mustard seed illustrates the point. "The kingdom of heaven is like a mustard seed, which a man took and planted in his field. Though it is the smallest of all your seeds, yet when it grows, it is the largest of garden plants and becomes a tree, so that the birds of the air come and perch in its branches" (Mt. 13:31-32).

In the Holy Land, "this little grain of mustard did grow into something like a tree... Jesus said his Kingdom was like the mustard seed and its growth into a tree. The point is crystal clear. The Kingdom of Heaven starts from the smallest beginnings, but no [one] knows where it will end..."[95] It is intended to grow and grow. It is intended that together Christians share in the advancement and increase of the kingdom of God's grace in and through the visible church of Jesus Christ.

The Methodology of Increasing

How does this increase in devotion, expression and in numbers takes place? First and foremost, we must affirm that in whatever we do, it is the Holy Spirit of God who makes increase possible. God gives the Spirit to all who believe in Christ (Jn. 3:34, Acts 2:38). The Holy Spirit *supernaturally* takes up residence in the believer's life (Jn. 14:17) and is our resource for increasing. Christ living within, by His Spirit, is that which enables us to crucify the lower nature of ourselves and develop Godly qualities (Gal. 2:20). It is *God* who causes the growth (Col. 2:19). We must cooperate with God's Spirit, however, in the endeavor.

Paul said we are not only *justified* by faith, but we are *sanctified* by faith as well. We are to live by faith, for the Christian life is by faith from the beginning to its end (Rom. 1:17). What does this mean? We are to decide to think and act with consideration of God in everything we do. We must decide to accept the responsibility for increasing. We must accept the challenge of becoming all we are intended to be in

---

[95] Ibid., 76.

Christ, and of accomplishing all that God has given us to do. In other words, personal *resolve* is needed.

God has gifted each one of us somewhat differently, although many of us share similar capacities and abilities. The Bible refers to our various abilities and capacities as *gifts* of the Spirit (see Rom. 12, 2 Cor. 12 and 1 Pet. 4). We grow spiritually as we identify the gifts of God to us and purpose to use them for his glory and the common good. We increase in the kingdom when we do the work of the Lord with the gifts he's imparted.

We should be engaged regularly in personal *devotional exercises*. Just as an athlete must practice and train for competition, so also the Christian is admonished to maintain a program of regular spiritual exercise. Thomas Watson said: "...take a turn, as it were, in heaven every day, by holy meditation,"[96] "... which will put a damp upon all worldly glory...which will promote holiness in us,...and which will be a spur to diligence."[97] We should pray often (1 Th. 5:17), study the Holy Scriptures (Heb. 5:12-14), think about and strive to improve in the various virtues identified for us in Paul's writings (Gal. 5, Col. 3).

The kingdom of God's grace is increased numerically when we intentionally *share the good news of Jesus Christ with others*. Faith comes from hearing the message (Rom. 10:17). When we accept the responsibility of being ambassadors for Christ (2 Cor. 5:20), the kingdom will increase. In these ways the years of our faithfulness will enable the kingdom of God's grace to increase within us and through us.

The Values of Increasing

Lastly, we shall mention briefly several of the values of spiritual growth. As we increase, we have greater *joy* in the Lord (Phil. 1:25). We have greater *discernment* to be able to distinguish good from evil, right from wrong, what is of God and what is not (Heb. 5:14, 1 Co. 2:14). Our faith becomes more firmly *grounded*, our position under God more

---

[96] Watson, 145.

[97] Ibid., 146.

solidly established (2 Pet. 1:10). We have a greater *sense of accomplishment* that we have contributed to the work of Christ on earth as it is already established in heaven. There is satisfaction in being productive and effective in God's work (2 Pet. 1:8). Increasing keeps us *focused* on the goal of our faith (Phil. 3:13-14); it keeps us moving in the right direction. Increasing develops *endurance* (Col. 1:11-12) and enables us to *persevere* to the close of our earthly journey. Since the kingdom of God's grace leads to the kingdom of God's glory, we should do all we can to increase, that we may not fall (Heb. 6:4-12, Rev. 2:4) and receive a rich welcome in the kingdom of God's glory (2 Pet. 1:11, Col. 1:11-12). As we increase, the ministry of Christ will increase, which is the ultimate objective of our entering and increasing in the kingdom of God's grace. These are values of increasing in the kingdom. We are called to increase the rule of God in our lives as we pass through this life on route to our final destination.

When we pray *thy kingdom come*, a part of what we mean is that we pray the kingdom of God's grace may be set up in our hearts, and that it may increase in us and through us. The process of increasing in the kingdom, of growing spiritually, inwardly, outwardly, and numerically, is an indication and validation of our calling; it provides the means of the kingdom's growth; and it is the method for the preservation of our election in the kingdom of God.

Chapter Eight

Imagining the Kingdom of God's Glory

Petition Two, Part Three

As Christians we look forward to the time, or to be more correct, the timelessness, of the rest of eternity when we shall be with Christ, when we shall be resurrected and, at the end of days, receive a rich welcome into the place Jesus has been preparing for us (Jn. 14:1-3). How well we increase in the kingdom of God's grace will have bearing on how fit we shall be for the kingdom of God's glory. Not only so, what we do as we increase in the kingdom will actually, according to 2 Pet. 3:11-13, hasten the coming of the kingdom of God's glory. Peter explained: "You ought to live holy and godly lives as you look forward to the day of God and speed its coming...we look forward to a new heaven and a new earth, the home of righteousness." Therefore, when we pray "thy kingdom come" we also mean the hastening of the coming of the kingdom of God's glory, the coming of the future realm, the there, the later, the not yet dimension of the kingdom of God. John Wesley expressed it this way: "We pray for the coming of his everlasting kingdom, the kingdom of glory in heaven, which is the continuation and perfection of the kingdom of grace on earth."[98] We need to ask, however, what is meant by the term glory. We know that by *kingdom* is meant the rule of God; and by *grace* is meant God's favor bestowed upon an undeserving humanity. What is meant by *glory*?

---

[98] John Wesley, 336.

Defining Glory

In Psalm 29 we read: "Ascribe to the Lord the glory due his name; worship the Lord in the splendor of his holiness...in his temple all cry, 'Glory!'" (29:2, 9). Psalm 19:1 says: "The heavens declare the glory of God; the skies proclaim the work of his hands." When Moses was in the presence of God on Mt. Sinai, the Lord said: "there is a place near me where you may stand on a rock. When my glory passes by, I will put you in a cleft in the rock and cover you with my hand until I have passed by. Then I will remove my hand and you will see my back; but my face must not be seen" (Ex. 33:21-23). In other words, Moses could not look at God's presence, his glory, straight on and live. When he descended from the mountain "his face was radiant" (Ex. 34:29) and he had to cover his face with a veil. In the Old Testament there are several Hebrew terms translated glory. *Kabodh* means honor or weight (Ps. 19:1). *Hadar* means excellent or majestic (Ps. 90:16). *Tohar* means purity or brightness (Ps. 89:44 KJV); *Sebhi*, prominent or conspicuous (Isa. 13:19); *addereth*, ample (Zec. 11:3); and *hodh* means grandeur (Job 39:20). In their various usages these words refer to qualities of God's essence, his nature, and his activities. English synonyms would be excellence, purity, brightness, prominence, grandeur. Such terms reveal and describe (albeit inadequately) God's presence and essence.

The New Testament term translated *glory* (Gk. *doxa* [from *dokeo*, to seem]), literally means a good opinion, an ascription, an estimate. To *glorify (doxazo)* God in the New Testament sense, therefore, means to suppose, that is, to suppose God to be great. It means to ascribe honor to God, to attribute to God the highest opinion or words of praise, to magnify, to extol God. In worship many Christians sing two such ascriptions of praise. One is called the *Doxology* (from *doxa*) and the other is named from its first two words in the Latin, *Gloria Patri* (Glory to the Father). Both are doxologies, sung ascriptions of high opinion to/about the triune God. The Old Testament and New Testament concepts of glory, taken together, therefore, suggest to us that the future kingdom of God's glory may be thought of as the *realm in the hereafter when and where believers will be in God's presence and when and where they will eternally praise his name.* God's presence and God's praise are what will characterize the kingdom of God's glory. To be *in Glory* will be being in the splendid presence of God where we shall praise him for his excellent greatness.

We must admit that any of our attempts to describe with human language the nature of the kingdom of God's glory are and will be inadequate. Although we try to conceptualize and imagine what the hereafter will be like, our thoughts and fantasizing will always fall short of the reality. And yet, God in his inspired scriptures has allowed us to catch a glimpse of glory through terminology and imaginings which help us be joyful about our destiny, and which characterizations of eternity motivate us to grow and persevere in the faith, and to serve God with fervor. Images of God's glory presented in the Bible include: *heaven*, the *Holy City/The New Jerusalem* (Heb. 11:10, Rev. 21:2), our Father's *house* (Jn. 14:2), and a better *country* (Heb. 11:16). We shall give attention to *heaven* since it is the reference most used in general conversation, and because the term is used in the Lord's Prayer. We will also discuss the *Holy City/New Jerusalem*.

Again, let us be honest and cautious at one point; that is, the portrayals of glory are simply that, portrayals, images. They are not literal descriptions, but imaginings. Having said that, we may also say with certainty, that images may not only be the most possible ways we may think about the hereafter; they may be the best ways for us humans, for they touch our whole being, our emotions as well as our minds. These images are God's gifts to us to help us fathom what is the spectacular nature of the kingdom of God's glory.

Heaven

It is a common expression in Christianity to think of the eternal destiny of believers as *heaven*. Christians believe they will *go* to heaven. What is meant by this term? When we pray the Lord's Prayer we begin: *Our Father in heaven...* We've explained previously that this phrase indicates that God is personal and approachable, as an earthly father should be to his children; and that God is holy, separate, other than that which is earthly. *Heaven* suggests his seat of authority, his place of honor, the abode of God, if you will. This is borne out by such references as 1 Kings 8:30, Solomon's payer of dedication before the altar in the newly constructed Temple. Solomon prayed: "Hear the supplication of your servant and of your people Israel when they pray toward this place. Hear from heaven, your dwelling place, and when you hear, forgive." In Luke 10:20 we read Jesus' words to some of his followers. He said: "...rejoice that your names are written in heaven." Jesus' parable of the Lost Sheep includes the following remark: "I tell you that in the same way there will be more rejoicing in heaven over one sinner who repents than over ninety-nine righteous persons who do not need to repent" (Lk. 15:7). To the Corinthians Paul wrote: "Now we know that if the earthly tent we live in is destroyed, we have a building from God, an eternal house in heaven..." (2 Cor. 5:1). And to the Philippians Paul declared: "...straining toward what is ahead, I press on toward the goal to win the prize for which God has called me heavenward in Christ Jesus" (Phil. 3:13-14).

Such citations are the basis upon which Christians have referred to the kingdom of God's glory as heaven. Confusion arises, however, when we read many of the 559 biblical references to heaven which do not seem to mean the same thing. Understanding the biblical usages on this matter will help us to arrive at a suitable definition of what heaven really means. For example, in the KJV Genesis 1:1 reads: "In the beginning God created the heaven and the earth." If we were to think of heaven as the abode of God, and possibly think the term *heaven* always refers to the abode of God, then we might ask where God's abode was before he created heaven. Similarly, in Revelation we read in chapters 21 and 22 of a new heaven and new earth. If God's abode is heaven, and God is perfect, and certainly God would not want to live in anything but a perfect house, we could ask what was wrong with the old heaven. I raise these questions to exemplify the kind of thinking people could have when they are unaware of how the term may be variously thought of and used in the Bible.

One of the problems with the rendering in the KJV of Genesis 1:1 is that it is inaccurate, or at least it misrepresents for modern readers what is intended in the account. In the NIV and most other versions of the Bible, the translation is "the heavens and the earth." So also in

Imagining the Kingdom of God's Glory

Psalm 19:1 we read: "The heavens declare the glory of God." Psalm 57:5 says: "Be exalted, O God, above the heavens." The Hebrew word *shamayim* is always a plural, although it is sometimes translated as singular. *Shamayim* literally means *lofty*. The New Testament Greek term *ouranos* means the *heights*. The ancient Hebrews conceived of multiple heavens. They believed the earth to be flat. Above the earth was the first heaven, the sky, our atmosphere, (e.g. Gen. 1:8-9, 20, Deut. 11:11, 2 Chr. 7:13, Prov. 23:5). Space above the sky, where the sun, the moon and the stars shine, is the second heaven (Gen. 1:15, 15:5; Job 9:9; Jer. 33:22). Above the heavens of sky and space was imagined the dwelling of God (1 Kings 8:22 & 30, 2 Kings 2:1-18, Ps. 57:5, Dan. 2:28, Mt. 6:9, 7:21). In the New Testament era the apostle Paul wrote in his second letter to the Corinthians: "I know a man in Christ who fourteen years ago was caught up to the third heaven. Whether it was in the body or out of the body I do not know—God knows" (2 Cor. 12:2). It was believed the heavens were hung, stretched out like a curtain (Isa. 40:22, Jer. 5:15, Ps. 104:2) and supported by massive pillars (Job 26:11, 2 Sam. 22:8).

Such a concept of the heavens or of the abode of God was inadequate, admitted even by those of the scriptures, for Solomon in his prayer mentioned above said: "The heavens, even the highest heaven, cannot contain you." The vastness and omnipresence of God yields such a response to thinking about where God may reside. From the point of view of the Bible, the third or highest heaven is the dwelling place of God. When we consider what is truly high for us in the United States, and what may be truly high for other peoples of the world, knowing the earth is not flat, but round, and when we realize that highness is a direction image, then what would be up for one region of the world would be down for another. We may safely conclude, therefore, that heaven is *beyond* us, that is, beyond our natural human powers of observation and perception.

Heaven as the highest of the heavens is an image of that which really is but which is most difficult to describe except in human and earthly terms. It is not difficult to imagine. We are not at a loss for concepts of the kingdom of God's glory, whether they be images of space beyond space or of city, or house, a better country, another shore, or whatever. We must be content with the images, their power to communicate, to soothe, and to lift our spirits in moments of doubt or despair and place us, as it were, into the dimension of God's kingdom of glory. Regarding heaven, we may conclude that it is where God is. *Going* to heaven means simply passing on to the *immediate presence* of God in the hereafter. Paul explained: "Our citizenship is in heaven. And we eagerly await a Savior from there, the Lord Jesus Christ, who, by the power that enables him to bring everything under his control, will transform our lowly bodies so that they will be like his glorious body" (Phil. 3:20-21). Heaven is where God is. Heaven is where Jesus and the angels are. Heaven is where believers will be, where we shall enjoy the presence of God, where we shall praise God, and through all eternity serve God in whatever ways he gives us. Heaven will be our reward (Mt. 5:12), our promised inheritance (1 Pet. 1:3-4).

The Holy City/The New Jerusalem

In Hebrews 11:8-16 we read of Abraham who was "looking forward to the city with foundations whose architect and builder is God..." John was given a vision of this city, the kingdom of God's glory. Revelation 21:1-4 reads:

> Then I saw a new heaven and a new earth, for the first heaven and the first earth had passed away. I saw the Holy City, the new Jerusalem, coming down out of heaven from God, prepared as a bride beautifully dressed for her husband. And I heard a loud voice from the throne saying, "Now the dwelling of God is with men, and he will live with them. They will be his people, and God himself will be with them and be their God. He will wipe every tear from their eyes. There will be no more death or mourning or crying or pain, for the old order of things has passed away."

Jerusalem for many centuries has been called the Holy City. It is supposed to be a city of peace, as its name implies. It is called the Holy City because that is where the Temple was located, where God met

Israel in the Temple's inner chamber, the Holy of Holies. Why, we may ask is the kingdom of God's glory called the New Jerusalem? To understand this it is valuable to know the classical Greek background of thought, particularly that of Plato's doctrine of ideas or forms which shaped many writers' thought during the early Christian era. "[Plato] thought that in the invisible world there existed the perfect form or idea of everything on earth, and that all things on earth were imperfect copies of the heavenly realities."[99] The New Jerusalem, the heavenly City of God, therefore, is the way God enabled John to conceptualize the perfect, ideal, promised environment and community in the hereafter. This meaning is further suggested by the measurements of the City given in Revelation 21:15-16.

> The angel who talked with me had a measuring rod of gold to measure the city, its gates and its walls. The city was laid out like a square, as long as it was wide. He measured the city with the rod and found it to be [about 1500 miles] in length, and as wide and high as it is long.

A city that has the same dimensions for its length, width, and height is the shape of a perfect cube. The New Jerusalem is envisioned as foursquare. Barclay explains:

> [It was common enough for cities in the ancient world] to be built in the form of a square; both Babylon and Nineveh were like that. But the Holy City was not only square; it was in the form of a perfect cube. The length, breadth and height were the same [dimensions]. This is significant. The cube was the symbol of perfection. Both Plato and Aristotle refer to the fact that in Greece the good man was called 'four-square' (Plato, *Protagoras* 339B; Aristotle, *Nichomachean Ethics* 1.10.11; *Rhetoric* 3.11). It was the same with the Jews. The altar of the burnt offering, the altar of the incense, and the High Priest's

---

[99] William Barclay. *The Revelation of John*, Vol. 2 (Philadelphia: The Westminster Press, rev. ed., 1976), 199.

breastplate were all in the form of a cube (Exodus 27:1; 30:2; 28:16). Again and again this shape occurs in Ezekiel's visions of the new Jerusalem and the new temple (Ezekiel 41:21; 43:16; 45:2; 48:20). But most important of all, in Solomon's temple the Holy of Holies was a perfect cube (1 Kings 6:20). There is no doubt of the symbolism which John intends. He intends for us to see that the whole of the holy city is the Holy of Holies, the dwelling-place of God [where believers will share in the blessedness of immediate fellowship with God].[100]

Moreover, we've quoted Revelation 21:3 which says: "Now the dwelling of God is with men, and he will live with them." The KJV rendering reads: "Behold, the tabernacle of God is with men..." The term used for *dwelling* (NIV) or *tabernacle* (KJV) [Gk. *skene*] literally means *tent*. The meaning is clear. In the wilderness the ancient Israelites were instructed to build a Tabernacle/Tent of Meeting where God would meet Israel and dwell with his people. In the New Jerusalem, therefore, we have an imagery which suggests that God will give his immediate presence to the saints forever. The kingdom of God's glory, therefore, is called the New Jerusalem because it will be there that believers will be in the immediate presence of God (Rev. 21:22 & 22:3-5).

Furthermore, if the dimensions of the Holy City given in Revelation were to be taken literally, they would amount to a city in the shape of a perfect cube of 2,250,000 square miles, a city with an area which would stretch from New York City across the Atlantic to London, England. Again, the point is crystal clear. By this symbolism we understand the Holy City will be large enough to hold as many people as needed. There will be enough rooms (Jn. 14:1-3) for all the faithful of the ages. The Holy City will be beautiful beyond imagination, a perfect environment. God's presence will be the light (Rev. 21:10-11). It will be a place of comfort, free of sin, free of death, grief, crying and suffering. It will be a place of service (Rev. 22:3) and of unending joyous worship (Rev. 22:9).

---

[100] Ibid., 211-212.

Imagining

Imagining the kingdom of God's glory is God's gift to us, that we may pass through life's journey with hope. From this we may understand in part the value of contemplation, of making time in our daily routine to think, to imagine, to dream, to wonder, to pray. Imagining our destination can help us guard against giving in to the temptations of the world. Reflection assists in motivating us to want to increase in the kingdom, to grow in faith so that we shall persevere and not fall. It keeps us on the right track of living and enables us to be more fit for heaven. Dwelling on the hereafter spurs us on to share the gospel with others, especially with those we long to enter the kingdom. Attention to the biblical images and those presented in our hymns brings joy, lifts the spirit, gives encouragement for the present, spiritual medicine for our afflictions, hope for the hereafter. It yields what Thomas Watson called a "gospel antidote,"[101] an easement of the sting regarding passing from this life, for "it is but a short flight, but an eternal triumph."[102] With Charles Wesley (1707-1788) we might pray:

> Finish then thy New Creation,
> Pure and spotless let us be;
> Let us see Thy great salvation
> Perfectly restored in Thee:
> Changed from glory into glory,
> 'Till in heaven we take our place,
> 'Till we cast our crowns before Thee,
> Lost in wonder, love and praise.

---

[101] Watson, 150.
[102] Ibid., 149.

Chapter Nine

Passing Into The Kingdom of God's Glory

Petition Two, Part Four

In an issue of *Our Daily Bread*, there was a devotional entitled "The Sting." Dr. M. R. DeHaan wrote:

> Years ago, while I was walking with my two young boys, a bee stung the elder of the two just above the eye. He quickly brushed it away and threw himself in the grass, kicking and screaming. No sooner had the bee been brushed away when it went straight for the younger son and began buzzing around his head. He tried to hide in the tall grass and began screaming for help. I picked him up and told him not to worry—the bee had lost its stinger. This particular bee can sting only once. It leaves its stinger in the victim and becomes harmless. So I took my younger son over to his older brother and showed him the little black stinger in his brother's brow. I told him, "The bee can still buzz and scare you, but it is powerless to hurt you. Your brother took the sting away."[103]

In this chapter we're going to linger a bit on a subject not necessarily a part of the interpretation of the petition. However, it is a logical and important matter to include: our *passing* from the kingdom of God's grace to the kingdom of God's glory. We're going to discuss the differences between the sting, the stinger, and the buzz of dying, for God has provided the means for overcoming, or at least reducing, moderating, diminishing, softening and subduing the fear and sting of dying. The main point we shall be making is: *Although death approach-*

---

[103] *Our Daily Bread* Vol. 42, No. 1 (Grand Rapids: RBC Ministries, April 11, 1997 entry).

es, *for the Christian the promise of the resurrection and God's resources help ease its sting.* We shall consider what the Bible says happens after we die; what will take place when Christ returns; and what resources God provides to ease the apprehension of dying.

After Death

In the Old Testament the term which describes the realm of departed spirits is *sheol*. Sometimes a passage which includes this Hebrew word unfortunately may have been rendered *grave*. It is unfortunate to be translated *grave* because a grave seems lifeless and final. Sheol is the Hebrew conceptualization for the region of departed human spirits who are conscious, either in bliss or in torment. As an example, in the prophecy of Isaiah, the prophet portrays unfaithful and exiled Israel as taunting the fallen king of Babylon who had previously enslaved the people of God. Isaiah forthtold (14:9-10): "[Sheol][104] below is all astir to meet you and your coming; it rouses the spirits of the departed to greet you...you have become like us." The picture here is one of *activity*. The departed are *conscious*.

Another example is found in Ezekiel's prophecy, where he spoke for God regarding the fate of the city of Tyre, to be overthrown by Nebuchadnezzar, King of Babylon. Ezekiel spoke: "This is what the Sovereign Lord says: 'When I make you a desolate city...I will bring you down with those who go down to the pit [Heb., *sheol*],... and you will not return to take your place in the land of the living.'" (Ezek. 26:19-20). Here *sheol* is the realm of the departed who are in disgrace.

Genesis 15:15 speaks of God's promise to Abraham that he would be gathered to his fathers in peace. Sheol, therefore, is also the Old Testament conceptualization for the realm of the departed who are in a state of God's blessing and grace. As we shall see, however, sheol is not the eternal home of the departed. David, in Psalm 16:9-10 declared: "...my heart is glad and my tongue rejoices; my body also will rest

---

[104] For *sheol* the NIV says *grave*. The KJV renders it *hell*, which is problematic since hell is the final destination, whereas sheol seems to be an intermediate state.

secure, because you will not abandon me to the grave [sheol]..."[105]

In the New Testament we find the Greek term *hades*, which may be viewed as equivalent to the Hebrew *sheol*. *Hades* is sometimes rendered *hell*, but this is not appropriate since *hell* (Gk. *gehenna*) is the final destination of the departed unrighteous. Even more clearly in the New Testament with the references to *hades*, we see the development of two possible destinies for the departed. We shall look to Jesus' story of the fates of the rich man and Lazarus as recorded in Luke 16:19-31 as our primary reference.

> There was a rich man who was dressed in purple and fine linen and lived in luxury every day. At his gate was laid a beggar named Lazarus, covered with sores and longing to eat what fell from the rich man's table. Even the dogs came and licked his sores. The time came when the beggar died and the angels carried him to Abraham's side. The rich man also died and was buried. In hell [Gk. *hades*] where he was in torment, he looked up and saw Abraham far away, with Lazarus by his side. So [the rich man] called to him, 'Father Abraham, have pity on me and send Lazarus to dip the tip of his finger in water and cool my tongue, because I am in agony in this fire.' [fire seems to be more figurative here than literal]. But Abraham replied, 'Son, remember that in your lifetime you received your good things, while Lazarus received bad things. But now he is comforted here and you are in agony. And besides all this, between us and you a great chasm has been fixed, so that those who want to go from here to you cannot, nor can anyone cross over from there to us.' [In other words, what's done is done.]

One view of this story interpreted by J. Allen Miller (1866-1935) is that hades (the New Testament equivalent of *sheol*) is the realm of the departed human spirits; that they are conscious, aware; that there

---

[105] The KJV renders this, "will not leave my soul in hell," which is inaccurate because hell, as we understand it elsewhere in scripture (e.g. Rev. 20:13-14), is not the equivalent of *sheol*. Hell [*gehenna*] is the final destiny where death and hades will be cast.

are (for the lack of more suitable terminology) two divisions or realms in hades, one in which the blessed of God are in peace; and one in which the condemned are in mental and emotional, if not also in physical torment, realizing their fate.[106] To the believer, the state beyond death has become an existence of tranquility. For the unfaithful, death's sting is real and everlasting. According to Miller's interpretation, sheol/hades is where conscious, departed spirits reside until the time appointed by God for the consummation of human history. Hades/sheol is an intermediate state between life as we know it now, and the promised resurrection of the elect of God, and/or the judgment of the unfaithful of the ages.

In these developing concepts of the afterlife in the Bible it is difficult to be dogmatic about all of the particulars, especially when the concepts are presented in story form. In this writer's view, it is helpful to recall the New Testament teaches that the elect will be in the presence of their redeemer in this intermediate state. Paul, in his letter to the Philippians stated emphatically: "I desire to depart and be with Christ" (Phil. 1:23). In his second letter to the Corinthians (5:8) Paul explained that being away from the body meant he would be at home with the Lord Jesus Christ. And Jesus, himself, while hanging on the cross, declared to the believing thief hanging next to him, "...today you will be with me in paradise" (Lk. 23:43), a reference to the realm of the departed faithful, with Abraham, Lazarus the beggar, and with all those whom God has included among the righteous. The realm in which Abraham was *far away* is that to which Jesus referred as *paradise*, what Miller described as the believers' "division" of hades. In the Bible's progressive revelation of these matters, it seems appropriate to reserve the term *hades* only for the unbelieving awaiting the judgment.

What happens after we die? Our bodies will have ceased to function; but the real us, the real you and me lives on. All departed human

---

[106] Dr. J. Allen Miller (1866-1935) was a former President of Ashland College and Dean of Ashland Theological Seminary. His teaching on hell is given in his *Christian Doctrine: Lectures and Sermons* (Ashland, Ohio: The Brethren Publishing Company, 1946), 284.

spirits are conscious and aware. Some will be in mental and emotional torment because of their unpardoned sin and unbelief. Many will be with Christ and in a state of tranquility and peace; but that is not the end of the story.

The Second Coming

The Bible also teaches that all departed spirits will face an ultimate and final destiny. The final events will take place when Jesus returns or after his reign, as we shall see. What does the scripture say?

First, Jesus promised to return. In John 14:1-3 we read Jesus' comforting words to the disciples. "Do not let your hearts be troubled. Trust in God; trust also in me. In my Father's house are many rooms; if it were not so, I would have told you. I am going there to prepare a place for you. And if I go and prepare a place for you, I will come back and take you to be with me that you also may be where I am." Jesus said he would return for the faithful.

Second, Jesus will return from the heavens. At his ascension the disciples "were looking intently up into the sky as he was going, when suddenly two men dressed in white stood beside them. 'Men of Galilee,' they said, 'why do you stand here looking into the sky? This same Jesus, who has been taken from you into heaven, will come back in the same way you have seen him go into heaven'" (Acts 1:10-11). Jesus will return, and will come from the heavens.

Third, at Jesus' return there will be the resurrection of the departed believers. That is, the departed faithful spirits will be clothed with new spiritual bodies. Matthew 24 speaks of the events at the close of human history, and of a period of great tribulation. "Immediately after the distress of those days...the Son of Man will appear in the sky...with power and great glory. And he will send his angels with a loud trumpet call, and they will gather his elect from the four winds, from one end of the heavens to the other" (Matt. 24: 29-31). Paul described this two-fold event of Christ's return and the resurrection of believers in 1 Corinthians 15:51-52. "Listen, I tell you a mystery: We will not all sleep [that is, not everyone will have died at his coming], but we will all be changed—in a flash, in the twinkling of an eye, at the last trumpet. For the trumpet will sound, the dead [meaning the departed believers] will be raised imperishable [given new spiritual bodies], and we [meaning those believers who are alive at his coming] will be changed [from physical to spiritual bodies]." Similarly Paul explained in 1 Thessalonians 4:14-17: "We believe that Jesus died and rose again and so we believe that God will bring [to heaven, understood] with Jesus those who have fallen asleep [the figure of speech for those who have died] in him...the Lord himself will come down from heaven, with a loud command, with the voice of the archangel and with the trumpet call of God, and the dead in Christ will rise first. After that, we who are still alive and are left will be caught up together with them in the clouds to meet the Lord in the air. And so we will be with the Lord forever."

The nature of our spiritual bodies (1 Cor. 15:44) is unknown. However, 1 Corinthians 15:49 says that they will "bear the likeness" of Jesus' resurrected body. Mark 16:12 says they will have another form or a different constitution. And in his letter to the Philippians Paul explained: "Our citizenship is in heaven. And we eagerly await a Savior from there, the Lord Jesus Christ, who, by the power that enables him to bring everything under his control, will transform our lowly bodies so that they will be like his glorious body" (Phil. 3:20-21). Hallelujah!

What will happen when Christ returns? At Jesus' second coming departed believers will be resurrected and those faithful who are alive will be changed, and all those will be gifted with imperishable bodies.

Fourth, after the return of Jesus, at which time believers will be resurrected and/or changed, the Bible says there will be a one thousand year reign of Christ on the earth, commonly referred to as the *Millenium*. Revelation 20:4-6 pictures Jesus' reign (see also 1 Cor. 15:22-26). "[The departed faithful] came to life and reigned with Christ a thousand years. (The rest of the dead did not come to life until the thousand years were ended.) This is the first resurrection. Blessed and holy are those who have a part in the first resurrection. The second death [reserved for the unrighteous departed] has no power over them, and they...will reign with [Christ] for a thousand years." Following the return of Jesus and the resurrection of believers, our Lord will reign for one thousand years on earth as a statement of ultimate authority and triumph over evil.

Fifth, following the Millenium, a second resurrection will come, the resurrection of the departed non-believers from hades. This is the time of the Judgment. Revelation 20:12-14 says: "[They] were judged according to what they had done...death and Hades gave up the dead that were in them...then death and Hades were thrown into the lake of fire. The lake of fire is the second death [hell (Gk. *gehenna*) is a synonym for the lake of fire]." So hades and departed non-believers are cast into hell, the final destiny of the unrighteous of the ages. The Bible closes the story by describing a new heaven and a new earth for the righteous, which is the dwelling place Jesus is preparing (Rev. 21).

We see the Bible teaches there are two destinies awaiting humanity. After the death of believers, their spirits are with Christ in the tranquility realm of paradise, an intermediate state between this life and the resurrection, a state of activity, consciousness, awareness and peace. After the death of non-believers, unfortunately their spirits are conscious and aware as well and in the torment of their condition awaiting the judgment of God. Which would you prefer?

Removing the Stinger

This brings us to two final points. The first is this: for those who have never given their hearts to God, by committing their lives to Jesus Christ, God's Son, the One who offered his life upon the cross of Calvary as an atonement for their sins, then the stinger of death is real; they are stung and they will be stung because of their sin and failure to acknowledge Jesus Christ as the Savior of their souls and the Lord of their living. Their destiny is a gloomy one, for they will be judged of God and eternally punished in some way; and I wouldn't want to wish facing death in that state on anyone. The only way the stinger can be removed is by recognizing that Jesus bore our sins upon the cross; and when we give our hearts to him, he removes the stinger from our heart's brow and positionally in God's view the debt we owe, due to our selfishness and sin, will have been paid. All who have never genuinely repented and asked the Spirit of Jesus Christ to come into their lives are encouraged here to do just that, through an act of prayer and resolve. By faith in Jesus, our brother, the stinger is taken away.

Easing the Sting

The second matter is this. For the believer, though the stinger has been removed, death still buzzes around to scare us. We are vulnerable to the scare because we still inhabit this body and this world. We still sin, though hopefully increasingly less. The forces of the world often come crashing upon us. However, God has provided the means for Christians to experience a reduction of the fear of dying, if not an altogether overcoming of the fear. The extent of the minimizing of the scare will most likely be in proportion to our faith and faith living. Consider these suggestions.

Know the Holy Scriptures. Immerse yourselves in the written and preserved Word of God. As you do, the Holy Spirit will be your Comforter. Your spirit will be bathed in the glow of God's inspired and revealed truths. They will shape your thoughts and bring joy and peace to your inner being. The more we fill our minds with the things of God, the less room there will be for other thoughts.

Review the truths regarding the destinies we've surveyed. Knowing the goal of our salvation should propel us onward to greater faithfulness. Awareness of the fate of non-believers should help us guard against falling into sin's grip.

It may also be helpful for us to *consider the images the Bible provides for the passage* from the kingdom of God's grace to the kingdom of God's glory, such as departure/exodus. At the transfiguration recorded in Luke 9:30, "...Moses and Elijah, appeared in glorious splendor, talking with Jesus. They spoke about his departure, which he was about to bring to fulfillment at Jerusalem" (Gk. for departure is *exodus*). The believer's dying is a departure, an exodus from this mode of existence to another; it is not an end in itself.

Another image is that of a sailing ship. Paul said in Philippians 1:23: "I desire to depart and be with Christ." In Greek the term rendered depart in this verse, as A. T. Robertson translates it, means "to weigh anchor and put out to sea."[107] Here death is pictured as "setting sail, a

---

[107] Quoted in Erwin W. Lutzer's *One Minute After You Die* (Chicago: Moody Press, 1997), 52.

departure on that voyage that leads to the everlasting haven and to God."[108] The term may be used as well for striking camp, "loosening the tent ropes, pulling up the tent pins and moving on. Death is a moving on."[109] The suggestion is this: let these images console any who are apprehensive about their passing.

Finally, the suggestion and the provision God provides for the soothing of our spirits is *working for the Lord*. Paul encouraged the Corinthians: "Always give yourselves fully to the work of the Lord, because you know that your labor in the Lord is not in vain" (1 Cor.15:58). While we are in the body we are to make it our goal to please the Lord through the service we render unto Him (2 Cor. 5:19). In the work God blesses and encourages our spirits, and when combined with all of the other provisions, serves to ease the scare and drive away the buzz.

The strife, the battle for the future, is over, for the stinger, which represents the consequences of unpardoned sin, is removed by Christ's death and resurrection. Death can no longer claim us for eternity. Dying is not an end. For the believer it is the passage to the beginning of the rest of life eternal in the presence of the Lord. The buzz may remain somewhat, but with faithful living, study, reflection and service, we may approach the close of our earthly pilgrimage with confidence and assurance that the promise of the risen Christ will be kept. On that day we shall be with Him in paradise. Hallelujah!

---

[108] William Barclay. *The Letters to the Philippians, Colossians, and Thessalonians.* rev. ed. (Louisville: The Westminster Press, 1975), 28.

[109] Ibid.

Chapter Ten

Doing God's Will

Petition Three

We've all heard of persons who, in difficult circumstances, when their proverbial backs were against the wall, have prayed something like: "Oh God, if you help me, I'll do whatever you want me to do." The prayer of the truly sincere individual (and only God knows the heart) may be honored by the Lord and granted. However, is this the way we should think about God's will? Isn't it true that such praying is really a desire to have God do what we would like for him to do, rather than a humble resignation to whatever God's will for us may be? On what scriptural basis may we believe we may manipulate God? Are we willing to fully surrender our lives to what God may will for us, without trying (as if we could) to maneuver God into accepting our terms?

A missionary to China, Betty Scott Stam, was someone who had surrendered her life to God's will. At one point she and her husband John were arrested by the communists, stripped, and marched through the streets of their village. Betty was forced to watch as John was decapitated. Then she was beheaded. Years before her martyrdom, Betty wrote the following prayer: "Lord, I give up all my own plans and purposes, all my own desires and hopes, and accept thy will for my life. I give myself, my life, my all utterly to thee, to be thine forever. Fill me and seal me with thy Holy Spirit. Use me as thou wilt. Send me where thou wilt, and work out thy whole will in my life at any cost, now and forever."[110]

A part of what is meant when we pray *thy will be done* is the surrendering of our whole lives to whatever is God's will for us, yielding to God his right to do as he wills. That might mean we pray for things we

---

[110] Philip Graham Ryken. *When You Pray: Making the Lord's Prayer Your Own* (Wheaton, Illinois: Crossway Books, 2000), 101.

may not want, for receiving *your will be done* might lead to suffering, even death.[111] Is it not a risk in a sense to pray this petition of the Lord's Prayer? Is it a risk not to pray it?

What *is* God's will that we pray may be done? And how is it done in heaven? We have a great task ahead of us, because there is more to this petition than we might think initially. To answer these questions we will need to examine the *scope* of God's will, and then reflect on the *manner* in which Jesus indicated God's will is to be done.

The Scope of God's Will

The New Testament word translated *will* (*thelema*) stresses not the act of willing so much as what is willed.[112] Therefore, one of the emphases of the petition is that which God has willed may be fulfilled on earth as it is in heaven. This refers broadly to God's kingdom, God's rule. As God's rule is carried out in heaven, so may it be internalized and actualized in peoples' lives. We may ask: What has God willed that should be fulfilled on earth? Another, amplified, and more specifically defined way of describing what God has willed, namely, that God's kingdom may come, would be to cite Paul's teaching in which he explained God's plan of the kingdom. To the Romans he wrote: "For those God foreknew he also predestined to be conformed to the likeness of his Son, that he might be the first-born among many brothers. And those he predestined, he also called; those he called, he also justified; those he justified, he also glorified" (Rom. 8:29-30).

Accepting the call of God and therefore being justified by God is another way of describing how persons enter the kingdom of God's grace. Being glorified may be understood as having both now and later aspects. Believers, following justification (entry into the kingdom), begin the process of becoming increasingly transformed into the likeness of Christ (Rom. 12:2, 2 Cor. 3:18). Believers are glorified partially and progressively in this life, and will be fully glorified in the hereafter (Phil. 3:21). The present journey of *becoming* is another way of saying believers are increasing in the kingdom.

---

[111] Ibid., 95.

[112] Frank Stagg, 115.

In his letter to the Ephesians Paul provided further clarification of God's plan.

> For he chose us in [Christ] before the creation of the world to be holy and blameless in his sight. In love he predestined us to be adopted as his sons through Jesus Christ, in accordance with his pleasure and will...In [Christ] we have redemption through his blood, the forgiveness of sins...he made known to us the mystery of his will...which he purposed in Christ...to bring all things in heaven and on earth together under one head, even Christ... In him we were also chosen, having been predestined according to the plan of him who works out everything in conformity with the purpose of his will...Having believed, you were marked in him with a seal, the promised Holy Spirit, who is a deposit guaranteeing our inheritance until the redemption of those who are God's possession...(Eph. 1:4-14).

The significance of the petition, therefore, is in part a prayer that the *plan* of God for the redemption of people and of the entire creation will be carried out and completed. In Ephesians 1 God's will (v.9) is synonymous with God's plan (v.11), "...not only in the present age [Gk. *aion*] but also in the one to come" (Eph. 1:21). Thomas Watson refers to this aspect of God's will as God's *secret will*, "the will of God's decree" for the plan of the ages, God's overall design for the history of the world.[113] Of course we must emphasize that the ultimate purpose of the plan is not merely the redemption of people and of the whole of creation. Such a plan has as its end bringing glory to God, that God may be exalted on earth as he is in heaven. Therefore, the *first* aspect of God's will is God's *predestined will*, the will of his planning. *May God's predestined will be accomplished.*

Certainly God's plan will be carried out whether we pray for it to be or not. Someone might ask, therefore: "What is the significance of our praying for it to be fulfilled?" We would answer that it is a kind of *lining up* of ourselves with God's plan, an expression of our desire and

---

[113] Watson, 151.

resolve to participate in the doing. It is an *offering of ourselves* to be of use to God in the carrying out of the plan, as in helping others to enter and increase in the kingdom. Therefore, we begin to understand that not only we as individuals, but together as the visible church of Jesus Christ, commissioned by him to proclaim the kingdom of God, are partners with God in the fulfillment of his purposes on earth. For truly God's will on earth is not done in most cases except through human agency. The doing of God's *predestined will* is certainly a major aspect of the meaning of this petition.

The *second* aspect of God's will implied in the petition is what we may call God's *prescribed will,* meaning God's *commands* which should be obeyed, the *decrees* which should be observed, the *ordinances* which should be lived out.[114] God's *prescribed will* is his general will for all people, a will revealed in the Holy Scriptures by which persons are guided to live holy lives. When we pray *thy will be done* in the prescriptive sense, we are praying for an active *conformity* in the world to God's precepts.[115] God has given the Law, common sense wisdom in the Proverbs, and numberless examples in scripture of what is right and wrong for human behavior. When we pray *thy will be done* we are praying that God's *predestined* will be carried out and that we may have a part in the doing of it; and we are praying that God's *prescribed* will for human behavior may be accepted and enacted more and more in the world generally, and by ourselves most definitely. In other words, we are praying that God's plan for the world be fulfilled and that his will for human behavior be accepted by more people everywhere and exemplified in us.

There is a *third* aspect to God's will. When we consider God's predestined will we realize that it takes people for God's plan to be carried out, people to introduce people to the kingdom of God. It takes people individually and collectively through the visible church to help others increase in the kingdom of God's grace. Therefore, there is a personal

---

[114] Ibid.

[115] Wesley referred to this as "active conformity to the will of God," 337.
Watson described it as "active obedience," 151.

dimension to that aspect of God's will. And when we think about the execution of God's prescribed will for human beings, it should be evident that it takes people to live the holy lives God intends for us to live. It should also be obvious that within each of the above, individuals not only have the prescribed directions from God's written word regarding appropriate general human behavior which glorifies God and brings health to societies, they also have *specific roles* to play in the fulfillment of God's will on earth. Some persons have more noticeable public leadership roles. Most have support functions. However, all Christians have an obligation to seek God's will for their personal lives, that they may assume their part in the conduct of God's predestined and prescribed wills, and that they may know the joys of a purposeful life lived in concert with what is God's will for them to be and do. The third aspect of God's will, therefore, is God's *personal will*, his will for us as individuals. We may identify at least three components to God's personal will.

One component would be our *lot in life*, so to speak, our general status, our race, nationality, physical stature and appearance, marital status, vitality, socio-economic level, and the like. To be content regarding God's will for us in these regards is needed since most of these aspects of our selves cannot change. Not to accept God's will for us can only bring discouragement and unhappiness throughout our days. God's personal will is that we "give thanks in all circumstances" (1 Th. 5:16).

A second component of God's personal will is the specific *work* which he may have predestined for us to do for his glory and for the carrying out of his overall plan for society. Naturally it is appropriate that all Christians seek to know God's will for their individual lives through an honest assessment of their abilities and interests, through the inner convictions and inclinations of the heart, through consultations with the Holy Scriptures and Christian advisors, and through a discernment of the circumstances in which we find ourselves. Learning to read the signs of God's direction is a worthwhile and important aspect of discovering God's will.

The third component is what we would call our *personal devotion-*

al orientation. Matthew Henry referred to this as "a life of devotedness to God...to refer ourselves to [God's] wise and holy directions and disposals, and cheerfully to acquiesce in them, and comply with them..."[116] It should be our duty "to have our eyes ever towards the Lord...[to] direct all to his honor...to acknowledge God in all our ways..."[117] This is what we mean by God's will for our personal devotional orientation.

Needless to say, internal conflict arises when we have difficulty accepting God's will for our personal lives, when we fail to accommodate our will to his. Some of us may not be personally satisfied with our lot in life, or what career we've found ourselves pursuing. We may have an uneasiness within because we've wanted to do other than that which has come to pass. In times of affliction or suffering we may have been angry and resentful or at least questioned why God permitted certain things to happen to us. Whatever the matter, as Christians we will be much happier and be a blessing to others if we allow ourselves to have a joyful resignation to God for the personal will which is his for us. Certainly Jesus is our model. When the time had come for his betrayal and eventual crucifixion, Jesus humbled himself in prayer before the Father and declared; "Yet not my will, but yours be done" (Lk. 22:42).

In sum, *may your will be done* is a petition that God's *predestined plan* for the redemption of people and of all creation be completed and that we will willingly participate in the fulfillment of it. It is also a prayer that God's *prescribed* will for human beings, his commands and intentions for human behavior, be accepted and enacted by people more and more all over the world, and especially by us. The petition is a prayer that God's will for our *personal* lives will be discovered, received, and accomplished with thankfulness and faithfulness, as we submit our wills to his.

---

[116] Matthew Henry. *The Secret of Communion With God* (Grand Rapids: Kregel Publications, 1991), 50 & 52.

[117] Ibid., 53-54.

The Manner of Doing God's Will

It would be fair to say that the phrase *as it is in heaven* may be applied to each of the first three petitions of the Lord's Prayer. Certainly our prayer is that God's name would be respected and revered on earth as it is in heaven; that God's rule would be established all over the globe as it is in the heavenly realm; and that God's predestined and prescribed wills will be carried out in the world as his will is obeyed and executed in heaven. What is done there is that which is accomplished by the *angels*. God's *name* is to be hallowed on earth as it is in heaven by the angels. God's kingdom is supposed to be established on earth in the same way as God's *rule* is maintained in heaven by the angels. God's *will* is intended to be carried out on earth as it is executed by the angels in heaven. The scriptural basis upon which such statements are made is given in Psalm 103:19-21.

> The Lord has established his throne in heaven,
>   and his kingdom rules overall.
> Praise the Lord, you his angels,
>   you mighty ones who do his bidding,
>   who obey his word.
> Praise the Lord, all his heavenly hosts,
> You his servants who do his will.

The angels, the psalm declares, are those heavenly beings who do God's will, a thought which is amplified and further clarified in the phrases *who do his bidding, who obey his word,* and *praise the Lord*. God's will in heaven is that he be praised and worshiped. This is further pictured in the scene in heaven presented in Revelation 7:11-12.

> All the angels were standing around the throne and around the elders and the four living creatures. They fell down on their faces before the throne and worshiped God, saying: 'Amen! Praise and glory and wisdom and thanks and power and strength be to our God for ever and ever. Amen!'

The worship of Jesus in heaven is also envisioned, as recorded in Revelation 5:11-12.

Then I looked and heard the voice of many angels, numbering thousands upon thousands, and ten thousand times ten thousand. They encircled the throne and the living creatures and the elders. In a loud voice they sang: 'Worthy is the Lamb, who was slain, to receive power and wealth and wisdom and strength and honor and glory and praise.'

Hebrews 1:14 says angels are ministering spirits. The angels ministered to Jesus in the garden (Lk. 22:42-43). One of their roles is to minister to those who will inherit salvation (Heb. 1:14). In heaven they do what God commands, obeying his word, performing the duties he declares for them, whatever they may be.[118] This three-fold will of God, praising God's name, obeying his word, and doing his bidding, an interesting parallel to the first three petitions of the Lord's Prayer, is what Christians should be doing on earth as it is in heaven. The question is, of course, how is God's will done by the angels in heaven? Understanding this will be the basis for knowing how the praising, the obeying and the doing are to be done on earth.

Of course, much of what we might say in answer to this question is speculative. None of us has been in heaven to know. And yet, if we were to cast the manner of our doing of God's will in the best possible light, we might come close to understanding how the angels do it, and, thereby, underscore how we should do it. We may identify eight ideas.[119]

We do God's will as the angels in heaven when we do it *regularly*, meaning without wavering, according to a set pattern of behavior (Ex. 25:40, Lev. 10:2). There should be a predictable order to our worship, for example; there should be discipline and regularity in our study; and there should be organization to our serving.

We do God's will as the angels when we accomplish it *entirely*, meaning thoroughly, leaving nothing out. John Wesley said *completely*.[120] "The angels in heaven do all that God commands; they leave

---

[118] Institutes, Vol. 2, III, XX, 43.

[119] Watson, 156-162.

[120] Wesley, 337.

nothing of his will undone" (Num. 15:40, Ps. 103:20, Acts 13:22, Heb. 1:14).[121] Watson offered a marvelous description of professed Christians who neglect doing God's will in its entirety.[122]

> Many do God's will by halves, they pick and choose in religion: in some they comply with God's will, but not in others; like a lame horse, which sets some of its feet on the ground, but favours one. He who is to play upon a lute, must strike upon every string, or he spoils all the music. God's commandments may be compared to a ten-stringed lute; we must obey his will in every command, strike upon every string, or we can make no good melody in religion. The badger has one foot shorter than the other; so hypocrites are shorter in some duties than others. Some will pray, but not give alms; some hear the word, but not forgive their enemies; others receive the sacrament, but not make restitution. How can they be holy who are not just? Hypocrites profess fair, but when it comes to sacrificing the Isaac, crucifying the beloved sin, or parting with some of their estate for Christ, they pause and say, as Naaman, 'In this thing, the Lord pardon thy servant.' (2 Kings 5:18). This is far from doing God's will as the angels do, God likes not such as do his will by halves. If your servant should do some of your work which you set him about, but not all, how would you like it?

We do God's will as the angels in heaven when we do it *sincerely*, meaning without pretending, "out of a pure respect to his command...with a pure eye to his glory...that God in all things may be glorified (1 Pet. 4:11).[123] We do God's will as the angels when we do it *willingly*, without complaining (1 Chr. 28:9, Ps. 110:3, 119:97, Jer. 15:16). We do God's will as the angels when we do it *fervently*, without slacking. The Apostle Paul exhorted: "Never be lacking in zeal, but keep your spiritual fervor, serving the Lord" (Rom. 12:11; see also Ps. 104:4).

---

[121] Watson, 157-158.

[122] Ibid., 158.

[123] Ibid., 15.

UNITED IN PRAYER

We do God's will as the angels when we give our best in every matter. We might translate *best* as that which is done *skillfully*, as in Psalm 33:3 (see also Gen. 4:3, Num. 18:19). Our service is as the angels in heaven when we do it *readily* and *swiftly*, that is, *obediently*, not questioning God's directions, serving without excuse (Ps. 18:44, Lk. 5:4). Our doing of God's will is as the angels when we do it *constantly*, never wearying of doing the work of God. The angels serve God "day and night" (Rev. 7:15), without interruption, and so should we.

To summarize, we do God's will on earth as it is done by the angels in heaven when we do it *regularly, entirely, sincerely, willingly, fervently, skillfully, obediently,* and *constantly*. That's quite a tall order, is it not? However, God is regular and constant, fervent, ready and willing in his attempts to help us be faithful. God's resources lack no enabling power to give us the attitudes and the competence needed for the accomplishment of his predestined, prescribed and personal wills. His angels as ministering spirits may be agents to assist us in some ways. Most certainly God's Holy Spirit is our Comforter and guide, our paraclete, as the KJV describes him, the one who goes alongside to help us (Jn. 14:16). It is the Holy Spirit who enables us to do God's will on earth as it is done by the angels in heaven.

So when we pray "thy will be done on earth as it is in heaven," we are praying that people everywhere, and especially disciples of Christ, may hallow God's name and worship him regularly and constantly on earth as the angels do in heaven. We are praying that people everywhere may willingly enter and sincerely strive to increase in the kingdom of God, readily studying God's written word and growing in his grace. We are praying further that people everywhere and Christians in particular will fervently participate in God's predestined and prescribed wills for humanity, and perform skillfully and completely the will of God for their personal lives.

All of the above is derived from *thy will be done on earth as it is in heaven*. Are we comfortable praying this petition? Because it includes and involves us in the doing of it, in the contributing to the carrying out of God's plan for the world, in the obeying of his prescriptions for human behavior, and in the assuming of what are our roles in his service, that God's will may be done in us and through us as it is by the angels in heaven.

Chapter Eleven
Depending on God
Introducing the Second Group of Petitions

It is usually in a crisis situation, during times of stress or suffering, that we acquire a heightened sense of dependence upon God. When our backs are against the wall, when we've lost our jobs, when there is little food for the table, when crops have been destroyed or the growing season has been shortened, that the words of the Lord's Prayer seem to come alive and relate to our lives: *O God, please give us our daily bread.*

When we've transgressed God's holy standard, hurt a neighbor and we're ashamed of it, whenever we've experienced not being forgiven by others and it hurts, the petition of the Lord's Prayer rings ever so clearly: *O God, please forgive our sins as we forgive those who sin against us.*

When we see how harmful it is to our selves and others to be caught in a morally compromising situation, when we've been brought to the brink of falling apart, when our character begins to crumble and our witness for God is shattered; when we've succumbed to the allurements of the world and the entanglements of the Evil One, when we've put ourselves, our possessions, our time and pleasures before God and the work of his kingdom, and realize how far away from God's intentions we've really strayed and how little we've accomplished for God's program in the world...then...then we understand more keenly what it means to pray: *O God, please, please lead us not into temptation and deliver us from evil.*

On the other hand, when life seems to be going well, when we're not seriously ill, when food is in abundance and we have enough money to buy the things we need and even those we desire; when we look at ourselves and say, "Well, I'm not as bad as so-and-so;" or "I've not done anything really bad lately;" how predictable it seems we, even as Christians, loose the edge of our human situation; how easy it is for us to slack off regarding personal devotions or worship attendance. We *neglect* to thank God enough for all that we have. Moreover, when we experience plenty, we are less inclined to ask God for our daily bread. We forget that it is not we who are in the control of ourselves; but that we are truly dependent upon God at all times.

We might ask, from a good motivation: Why should we ask God for our daily needs when we have them? What right do we have to keep asking God for ourselves, when there are so many who have greater needs? By what right do we as sinful creatures have to expect God will grant anything?

These issues of dependency and rights, and, as we shall see, responsibilities, are those we need to address generally before we can more specifically discuss the meanings of each of the second group of three petitions of Jesus' prayer.

The first three petitions should not surprise us regarding their content. For disciples of Jesus it seems quite appropriate to pray for God's name to be honored and revered. It is consonant with the Gospel to pray that people all over the world enter and increase in the kingdom of God's grace, and that they may persevere in the faith as they look forward to their translation into the kingdom of God's glory. It is absolutely and squarely correct and fitting for believers to pray that God's predestined, prescribed and personal wills be realized and fulfilled on earth as they are in heaven. These are lofty, God-honoring, God-serving, God-glorifying petitions.

With "give us this day our daily bread," the Lord's Prayer at first glance seems to change direction. From God's affairs the attention is directed to human needs, particularly those of disciples, for their daily bread, for forgiveness, for being spared severe trial, and for deliverance from evil and the Evil One. It is one thing to align ourselves up with God's program. Is it proper and acceptable for Christians to make such personal, self-serving requests? What right do we have to ask God for anything? If we do have the right, which it is clear we do because Jesus included such petitions in the prayer, then it would be helpful for us to examine the reasons why it is not only acceptable, but indeed necessary to follow the calls for God's work to be realized with *pleas* for personal helps. Moreover, it would seem beneficial for us to comment on the acceptability of the *manner* in which these petitions are presented; that is, in the *imperative*: *Give...Forgive...Lead us not...Deliver...* What right do we have to *command* God?

Reasons for the Right of Personal Petition

The first reason why we may petition God for human needs is because the prayer which Jesus offered is the type of prayer which permits such requests. As we mentioned in the chapter on the Jewish setting of the Lord's Prayer, the *genre* of the Lord's Prayer is that of a "biblical *tephillah*—a prayer in the narrowest sense of the word: that is, a petitionary prayer."[124] Petitionary prayers occur in the Old Testament as parts of Psalms. Psalm 17:1, for example, reads: "Hear, O Lord, my righteous plea; listen to my cry. Give ear to my prayer—it does not rise from deceitful lips." Another example is seen in Psalm 86:1: "Hear, O Lord, and answer me, for I am poor and needy." Psalm 109:3-4 specifically mentions this type of prayer. David cried out to God: "With words of hatred [the wicked] surround me; they attack me without cause. In return for my friendship they accuse me, but I am a man of prayer [*tephillah*]." We have the right to petition God for personal concerns because God's inspired word, Jesus' words, indicates that petitionary prayer is an acceptable mode of addressing God.

We may say as well that the right is given to pray for daily bread, for forgiveness of sins, and for defense against temptation and the wiles of the Evil One, because we have first prayed for the fulfillment of *God's* interests, *God's* plan, *God's* program. Jesus taught: "Seek first [God's] kingdom and his righteousness, and all these things will be given to you as well" (Mt. 6:33). Our Lord's words help us remember to keep things in proper perspective. God's glory must come first above all things. To say it another way, we may petition God for important personal concerns because we've first aligned ourselves with God's affairs and accepted the co-laborship of God's work. To request the necessities of food, reconciliation, and fortification against trial and evil is appropriate because the ultimate objective of them being granted is to support the

---

[124] Alfons Deissler. "The Spirit of the Lord's Prayer in the Faith and Worship of the Old Testament," *The Lord's Prayer and Jewish Liturgy*, 4.

overall purpose for human life: the glorification of God. We would not be able to do God's work unless we were sustained physically, unless we were living in right relationship with God and with others, and unless there were divine assistance to keep us on the right behavioral track. In other words, what, at first glance, may seem to be self-serving requests, are really not as much as they are requests for the necessary supports for the accomplishment of God's purposes. We need to remember the prayer of Jesus was offered as *instruction* to disciples. In order to be effective as disciples, they needed, and we need help for the physical, spiritual and social aspects of our lives and ministries. There's an implied *connection* between God's *program* and the *provisions* needed for the well-being of disciples. John Calvin commented: "As the law [The Ten Commandments] of God is divided into two tables, of which the former contains the duties of piety, and the latter the duties of charity, so in prayer Christ enjoins us to consider and seek the glory of God, and, at the same time, permits us to consult our own interests."[125] "Again, in this prayer, our Lord first instructs us to seek the glory of God, and then points out, in the second part, what we ought to ask for ourselves."[126]

Moreover, because it is acceptable for us to approach God with personal requests, we understand God to be truly concerned about our lives in their entirety. After all, God's reputation is at stake! Not only so, he loves us, and desires to care for us. We need only to recall our previous remarks regarding God as Father. The Creator is not only the holy transcendent other, he is also our immanent caretaker, our provider. God is approachable as a faithful parent will be. "The Lord is good, a refuge in times of trouble. He cares for those who trust in him..." (Nah.1:7). "Cast all your anxiety on him because he cares for you" (1 Pet. 5:7).

In the fourth instance, we have the privilege of petitioning God because in doing so we are acknowledging our *dependence* upon God for all things. As the Apostle Paul proclaimed: "In [God] we live and move

---

[125] *Calvin's Commentaries* Vol. XVI, 316.
[126] Ibid., 332.

and have our being" (Acts 17:28). God is the *provider* of all our needs, those physical as well as those intangible. God is the donor. God is the *giver*, the *forgiver*, the *leader*, the *deliverer*. We are dependent upon God for all of life's needs and concerns. Calvin wrote: "...we give ourselves over to his care, and entrust ourselves to his providence, that he may feed, nourish, and preserve us."[127] Every good gift is from above (Jas. 1:17). Our God will meet all our needs according to his riches in Christ Jesus our Lord (Phil. 4:19). Thomas Watson offered a scriptural catalog of God's beneficence including wisdom (Isa. 28:26), riches (2 Chr. 1:12; Deut. 8:18), peace (Ps. 147:14), health (Jer. 30:17; Ps. 6:2), rain (Job 5:10), and our daily bread (Prov. 30:7-8).[128]

When we acknowledge our dependence upon God we attribute all we have and are to him as the primary cause of all benefits. Too often people ascribe praise to secondary causes and forget God.[129] At one time or another we may hear someone being referred to as a self-made person. How sad it is when no credit is given to God for enabling the individual to achieve certain goals. How wonderful and appropriate it would be for someone in such a station in life to attribute all of his/her success to the hand of God. Credit should be given where credit is due. Moses' words to the Israelites are worth remembering: "You may say to yourself, 'my power and the strength of my hands have produced this wealth for me'. But remember the Lord your God, for it is he who gives you the ability to produce wealth..." (Deut. 8:17-18). Matthew Henry commented on this truth of the ultimate cause of our well-being when he wrote:

> To be religious is to enjoy God in all our creature comforts...It is to take the common supports and conveniences of life, be they often richest or be they of the meanest kind, as the products of his providential care concerning us, and the gift of his bounty to us...It is to look above second causes to the first

---

[127] *Institutes*, Vol. 2, III, XX, 44.
[128] Watson, 195.
[129] Ibid., 197.

cause, through the creature to the Creator, and to say concerning everything which is agreeable and serviceable to us, 'This I asked, and this I have from the hand of my heavenly Father'.[130]

God is our great benefactor. God is the donor, our provider. Upon him we are dependent. He gives the ability with which anything good is accomplished in and through us.

Someone may say: If we already have what we need in terms of food and other day-to-day necessities, why should we bother God with such requests? It is not really a selfish motivation which prompts us, as Jesus taught, to petition God for "our daily bread" when we have a sufficient supply. We pray as a way of seeking God's continuance. Occasionally we are reminded how fragile life and the human circumstance really are, how dependent upon God we are at all times. All that we are and have can be swept or blown away in an instant. We have the right and the opportunity to pray for our everyday needs because in so doing we are *petitioning God for a continuance of his provisions and supports.*

Furthermore, to petition God in this way is also a means of *thanksgiving*. Even when our earthly needs are met, it is proper for us to pray for them because in so doing we show forth our gratitude to him whose love has been showered upon us, in little and in much. To refrain from praying would actually be a shortcoming on our part, an insult to God, an indication we've taken God's provisions for granted. God is honored when we regularly offer our respectful requests and thanks in prayer.

Another reason why we have the right and even the obligation to pray for human concerns is because of the *responsibility* which is attached to each petition. The *collective, plural* nature of the Lord's Prayer (give *us* this day *our* daily bread; forgive *us our* sins, as *we* forgive *those* who sin against *us*; lead *us* not into temptation, but deliver *us* from evil) suggests that our petitions are not merely for individual, self-serving concerns or wants; but also for the provisions needed for others, particularly for disciples, our fellow Christians; for we are responsible as agents of God and disciples of Jesus to see to it that others have their

---

[130] Matthew Henry, *The Pleasantness of a Religious Life*, 50-51.

daily bread. We are obligated to forgive others any wrongs committed against us. We must guard against leading others into difficult or morally compromising circumstances, and help protect fellow Christians in particular from the entanglements of that which is evil in the sight of God. In other words, a *genuine regard* for others is what our Lord requires of us.

The direction to forgive others is given not only within the prayer, but also in the remarks of Jesus which follow it in Matthew 6:14-15: "For if you forgive men when they sin against you, your heavenly Father will also forgive you. But if you do not forgive men their sins, your Father will not forgive your sins." These are sobering words, added commentary by Jesus which makes us shudder. They cause us to stop in our tracks and examine our motives when we pray, and how we deal with our fellow human beings, especially when we've been wronged by them in any way. Further comment and interpretation on this particular subject will be offered in the chapter devoted exclusively to that petition.

In addition to these words of admonition which tie together receiving forgiveness with forgiving others, all of the *plurals* of the prayer provide a *qualification* for our prayers for human concerns and which emphasize a *responsibility* on our part toward others. The collective nature of these petitions suggests Jesus emphasized the communal nature of Christianity and the relational character in general of all life as in "as we forgive those" who may be anyone, Christians and non-Christians alike. This communal nature is characterized by two very important aspects: that human beings in general and God's family of faith (the Israelites and the Christians) in particular were and are intended by God to be and live intentionally mutually dependent upon him in and for all things; and that human beings in general, and God's people in particular are intended by God to live interdependent with each other. *Mutual dependence* upon God and human *interdependence* are the thoughts behind the plurals in the Lord's Prayer. We are "fellow citizens with God's people and members of God's household..." (Eph. 2:19). The Moffatt translation of Philippians 3:20 says we are a "colony of heaven." We are admonished: "Do nothing out of selfish ambition or vain conceit, but in humility consider others better than yourselves. Each of you should look not only to your own interests, but also to the interests of others" (Phil. 2:3-4). John wrote: "If anyone has material possessions and sees his brother in need but has no pity on him, how can the love of God be in him?" (1 Jn. 3:17). We are to "submit to one another out of reverence for Christ" (Eph. 5:21). "Be kind and compassionate to one another, forgiving each other, just as in Christ God forgave you" (Eph. 4:32). What is at stake, of course, is the hallowing of God's name, the entering and increasing of persons in God's kingdom, and the doing of God's will. The extent to which we as Christians are faithful and successful in living mutually dependent upon God and harmoniously interdependent with each other will be determinants for the success of our hallowing, our entering and increasing and persevering, and our doing of God's will.

To review, the reasons why we have the right to approach God in prayer with personal petitions are: because *petitioning prayer* is permitted, as Jesus instructed; because we've kept matters in *proper perspective* by praying for the honoring of God and the fulfillment of his purposes on earth first of all; because in praying we acknowledge that God *cares* for us; because in such petitions we recognize before God our *dependence* upon him for all things; because such prayers are the way we ask God for a *continuance* of his supply; because in praying for our needs we are *giving thanks* to the Lord for all his benefits; and because the petitions are not merely self-serving. Attached to each petition is an *implied responsibility* each disciple must assume for the well being of others. As Arthur Dyck has articulated it: "Individual life is not actually something that comes solely by having a living body of one's own but as a state of interdependence, maintained by a human network of aid, services, and restraints."[131] There is a social dimension and responsibility linked to each petition.

---

[131] Arthur Dyck, *Rethinking Rights and Responsibilities: The Moral Bonds of Community* (Cleveland: The Pilgrim Press, 1994), 6.

The Manner of Request

One further matter remains at this point in this introduction to the second group of petitions; namely, the manner in which it is given us to petition. We might ask: What right do we have to use the imperatives: *give…forgive…lead us not…deliver us…*? What right do dependent creatures have to order or command their Creator? The short answer would be that the use of imperatives is consistent with petitionary prayer, as illustrated above in the Psalm references. Another reason might be that such bold and seemingly presumptuous usages are possible because disciples are permitted and commanded to concern themselves with the fulfillment of God's purposes in the world.[132] If God expects us to be engaged in his work, then we have the right to hold God to his word, if you will, and rely upon his providing for our needs.

A further possible interpretation for the use of the imperatives is that considering the acute needs for God's will to be done in the world and the need for God's plan to be realized in peoples' lives, there is an *urgency* which seems to be conveyed in the Lord's Prayer. It is almost as though there is an urgent *please* which could be inserted into each phrase, and offered as though the petitioner were on bended knee. Realizing that God is the understood subject of each request, we might recast each to say:

> Oh God, *please give* us what is needed for this day of life and service. As you have given in the past, please continue to provide what we need to do your will. Oh God, *please forgive* us our sins, as we have forgiven the sins of those who have sinned against us, that we may be in right relationship with you and them, and thereby, be in an appropriate frame for glorifying you, making you known, and doing your will. Oh God, *please do not test* us beyond that which we are able to bear; *please protect* us from the wiles of the Evil One; place a hedge around us, a mighty fortress, that we may not succumb to the ways of the world.

---

[132] Barth, *Prayer*, 67.

UNITED IN PRAYER

The usage of the imperative is not an attempt on our part to command or order God. How could we do that! Rather, *give, forgive, lead not*, and *deliver* us are *urgent pleas* for God's help, that we may be equipped, sustained, and fortified for all that which is expected and required of us as disciples. The tasks are great. The challenges are awesome. The risks are numerous, the stakes are high: the souls of the human race!

Chapter Twelve
Requesting Daily Provisions
Petition Four

Have you noticed how many restaurants serve the most delectable yeast rolls? Isn't it an almost indescribably wonderful experience to begin one's dining event with fresh-baked, heavenly-smelling, warm and buttery bread? There's something about bread which is special. It tastes great, and seems to be the basis or an essential for many meals. In the tradition of what we refer to as *breaking bread* with others, bread is a symbol of the fellowship shared. Of course, our Lord gave bread a special significance when he used it to represent his body which would be broken for the sins of all who would bend the knee of their hearts and surrender their lives to God, thus enabling fellowship with the Father to be restored.

In this chapter we are going to interpret the meaning of *bread* in the fourth petition, then consider the significances of the terms *this day* and *daily*.

Interpreting Bread

Throughout the history of the Christian Church a number of possible meanings have been offered for the term *bread* in the fourth petition of the Lord's Prayer. For example, recalling the words of Deuteronomy 8:3, a reference which Jesus quoted (Mt. 4:4) when challenged in the desert by the Evil One, "Man does not live on bread alone but on every word that comes from the mouth of the Lord," may we be led to believe *bread* in Jesus' prayer refers to the spiritual fortification provided by the *scriptures*?

Another interpretation offered is that bread is a reference to internal *spiritual nourishment* generally, the intangible divine strength for life which only God can provide. Church Fathers such as Augustine viewed the bread this way.[133] Allegorizing was the method of interpretation of

---

[133] Augustine, 41.

later theologians as well. John Wesley, for example, applied both physical and spiritual meaning to bread when he wrote: "By bread we may understand all things needful, whether for our souls or bodies...the things pertaining to life and godliness...not barely the outward bread...but much more the spiritual bread, the grace of God, the food which endureth unto everlasting life."[134] Should we consider bread in the Lord's Prayer as spiritual nourishment, or perhaps, inclusively as both the tangible and intangible food needed for living?

Bread has also been described as a symbol pointing to *Jesus*. Biblical support for this viewpoint is given in the sixth chapter of the Gospel of John. "For the bread of God is he who comes down from heaven and gives life to the world" (6:33). Jesus also said: "I am the bread of life. He who comes to me will never be thirsty" (6:35; also 6:41, 51). May we think of bread in the Lord's Prayer as a symbolic reference to Jesus, the Bread of Life?

Yet another interpretation of bread is to view it as a reference to the *Eucharist*. As supportive of this sacramental explanation, adherents cite John 6:51: "I am the living bread that came down from heaven. If anyone eats of this bread, he will live forever. This bread is my flesh, which I will give for the life of the world." Paul's words in 1 Corinthians also relate: "For whenever you eat this bread and drink this cup, you proclaim the Lord's death until he comes" (1 Cor. 11:26). Is it proper to think of bread in the Lord's Prayer as referring to the remembrance of Christ's sacrifice?

We may ask: Is it appropriate to attribute to bread more than one meaning, since Jesus, particularly as the Gospel of John illustrates, used double meaning language in his teaching, using the earthly to represent the heavenly, for example, in his parables (e.g. "the kingdom of God is like a mustard seed.")? To his disciples, who encouraged Jesus at one point to eat something, our Lord replied: "My food...is to do the will of him who sent me and to finish his work" (Jn. 4:34). "...the one who feeds on me will live because of me" (Jn. 6:57). In Jesus' teachings, spiritual truths were often communicated in terms of the physical. So, it would

---

[134] Wesley, 338.

seem plausible to explore all the possible options of meaning, to be open to multiple explanations. While I would not want to dismiss all of the above as possible overtones for the bread of the Lord's Prayer, I believe we can settle on a direct meaning more likely and simply intended by Jesus, and that *that* basic meaning should be appreciated and valued.

What is the basic meaning of bread? The term *bread* (*artos*) in the Lord's Prayer is a figure of speech. Specifically, it is an example of a literary device known as *synecdoche*, where one thing stands for a whole class of things. Although food could be the whole of which bread is a part, we understand bread to be a symbol of all the *temporal* needs of human life. By temporal we mean mostly *those physical things or needs with which we are concerned in our everyday lives on earth.*[135] Included would be food, clothing, shelter, as well as the strength to do the tasks each day brings.

In the Lord's Prayer bread is used metaphorically, as a symbol of life's necessities. More than food, bread represents the many everyday provisions God makes available and which we need for our lives. We may ask: Why did Jesus choose bread to represent our temporal needs? Both in the Old Testament era and during the days of Jesus' ministry, bread was an example and the key symbol of God's providential care. Meals were considered sacred, symbols of God's supply for deliverance and sustenance both physical and spiritual. It was commanded by God to have bread on a special table in the Tabernacle as a sign of God's presence and provision (Ex. 25:30).[136] Within the Feasts of the Hebrews (e.g. Lev. 23:4-8) and the Lord's Supper, bread was and is used to signify God's provisions and redemption. Bread, from a biblical point of view, has always been considered something sacred, a symbol of God's pledge to care for us. Bread is not just an object, but has its meaning in the prayer as a pointer to the providence of God.[137]

We see, therefore, that the bread of the Lord's Prayer refers to and

---

[135] This figure of speech is discussed both by Calvin (*Calvin's Commentaries* Vol. XVI, 323) and Watson (203).

[136] See commentary on Leviticus 24:1-9 in George A. F. Knight's *Leviticus* (Philadelphia: The Westminster Press, 1981), 145-146.

[137] John Macquarrie. *A Guide to the Sacraments* (New York: Continuum, 1997), 20.

helps us appreciate all of God's kindnesses extended to us. Bread helps us realize how utterly dependent upon God we are for all things, and it underscores the fact that God is interested in our total welfare, not only our souls, but also our bodies. God cares about our bodily needs because he is the primary cause of our bodies coming into existence; and if we are to try to fulfill the directive of God to love God with all our hearts, souls, minds and strength (bodies), then we must come to the conclusion that God cares about our temporal needs. Because he does, and because we need to be sustained each day to hallow God's name, to increase in and advance the cause of the kingdom of God, and to accomplish God's predestined, prescribed and personal wills, we may pray: *Give us this day our daily bread.* Thomas Watson, in support of this interpretation, wrote: "Temporal things must be prayed for spiritual ends...Many pray for outward things only to gratify their sensual appetites...We must have a higher end in our prayers; we must aim at heaven while we are praying for earth...We must desire these things to be as helpers in our journey to heaven."[138] The bread we pray for, therefore, represents the temporal needs God supplies for our well-being, and for the doing of his will. We may say the scriptures invite us to have double vision, to see life for what it is, and what it may be for the glory of God.

A point which helps us guard against too fanciful an interpretation of bread was made by C. F. Yoder (1873-1955), a Brethren scholar of the early 1900's, who provided in his volume on the ordinances of the church a literal translation of the petition. His rendering was: "Give us for the coming day our little loaf."[139] Accepting this as a fair translation, since *artos* originally meant fragments or morsels of bread, we are led to believe the emphasis is really on the *basic, minimal* temporal needs for human life. It would be unlikely for Jesus to intend this petition to refer to Holy Communion, the scriptures, or general spiritual sustenance when using a phrase like a "little loaf." For certainly we

---

[138] Watson, 199.

[139] C. F. Yoder. *God's Means of Grace* (Elgin: Illinois: Brethren Publishing House, 1908), 101.

would not pray for a daily crumb of Jesus or just a small portion of God's precepts. Indeed, we should gorge on God all we can. We could never ingest enough! When it comes to things temporal, however, the *minimum* is what we should request; for, as we shall explore shortly, this petition includes a *limitation* on what we should request. We are to refrain from desiring excessive amounts of earthly goods. This meaning supports one of the overall concerns of the prayer; namely, our need to be *dependent* upon God for all things. The fact that our Father in heaven is genuinely concerned about our everyday welfare should prompt us to give thanks regularly for all his benefits. Bread is a reference to our basic necessities, the provisions which enrich our lives, sustain us, and enable us to accomplish God's will.

Limiting Acquisitions

The terms *this day* and *daily* in the fourth petition also suggest dependency. The definition of the term (*semeron*) rendered *this day* (KJV, NASB, NRSV, ESV) or *today* (NIV, JB, NLT) is straight forward enough. The request is made theoretically during a day and presumably during the earlier hours of a day. Calvin rendered it "day by day."[140] The term (*epiousion*) translated *daily* has been more difficult to render because it occurs only here in the entire Bible. Most versions render it daily. *Daily* (*epiousion*) is suggestive of continual action. We pray daily that our needs will be granted without interruption, ultimately so that we may glorify God without interruption. John Wesley wrote: "What is sufficient for this day; and so for each day as it succeeds...For we are to take no thought for the morrow. For this very end has our wise Creator divided life into these portions of time, so clearly separated from each other that we might look on every day as a fresh gift of God, another life, which we may devote to his glory."[141] The daily units of time serve to control and regulate our need for temporal things. Our Lord has placed a *limitation* or restraint upon us to help us in no less than the following ways. It helps us focus our attention more on him

---

[140] *Institutes*, Vol. 2, III, XX, 44.

[141] Wesley, 338 & 339.

rather than ourselves, to be more *God-centered* rather than self-centered, thus glorifying his name. The limitation helps us realize our *dependency* upon God for each day and for all we need. It coaxes us to guard against being greedy, against the excessive desire for material things. Each of these concerns is spoken to in Exodus 16 which tells of the Israelites' need for food when they were traveling in the desert following their deliverance from Egypt and the Red Sea. "I will rain down bread from heaven for you. The people are to go out each day and gather enough for that day. In this way I will test them and see whether they will follow my instructions...Each one is to gather as much as he needs..." (Ex. 16:4, 16).

God chose to regulate their supply of food and restrict their gathering to help check their proclivity for self-centeredness. God was forcing them to learn regular dependence upon him, and to restrain their natural inclinations to be greedy. God wanted them to think in terms of being less self-reliant and more dependent and temperate; to be less casual about everyday matters and more regular and intentional about appreciating God for all things; to be less interested in material things and more appreciative of the minimum as a way God is recognized as their daily provider. These messages are conveyed to us through the fourth petition of the Lord's Prayer, specifically through *this day* and *daily* taken together.

With respect to the matter of dependency, we need not be anxious about our needs. If we seek God's concerns first, he will honor our devotion and provide for all we need (Mt. 6:33-34). Concerning the matter of greed, we should be thankful that Jesus instructed us on this matter, because historically we know that those who covet more than they need sometimes engage in immoral acts, as the stories of Ahab (1 Kings 21:1-29, 2 Kings 9:4-10:11) and Ananias and Saphira (Acts 5) so vividly illustrate. Coveting is cast in scripture as a form of idolatry (Col. 3:5), the worship of things rather than the exaltation of God. Martin Luther, in the sixth stanza of his hymnic interpretation of the Lord's Prayer, expressed this:

> Give us each day our daily bread,
> And let us e'er be clothed and fed.
> From war and strife be our defense,
> From famine and from pestilence,
> That we may live in Godly peace,
> Free from all care and avarice.[142]

The antithesis of greed is contentment. Positively speaking, therefore, the petition is a call for disciples to be content with what God supplies, with what material goods we've been granted (Phil. 4:10-13).

To review, *Give us this day our daily bread* is a petition for human matters. However, it includes *limitations* on our acquisition of temporal needs. We may ask for our needs, but only as we do so with an eye toward *glorifying* God and doing his will. We are called to honor God daily by calling upon him for the things which sustain us physically as a sign of our respect and dependency upon God. We are encouraged to appreciate the *minimum* needed to sustain us, to guard against being greedy. Moreover, we should think in terms of assisting others who are less fortunate than ourselves. We should remember that it is only by God's grace that we have anything at all (Deut. 24:19-22).

Although some may not consider it so, there are advantages of not having an abundance of material things. Having the *minimum* leads us to give *thanks* to God more readily for what we do have. The minimum causes us to *approach* God daily through the spiritual disciplines, fostering regularity and constancy. This helps us focus on the more important aspects of life, upon soul food, the imperishable things. Watson said; "If God keeps us to a sparse diet, if he gives us less in temporals, he has made it up in spirituals..."[143] Having the minimum cultivates dependency upon and trust in God. Barclay noted: "It teaches us to

---

[142] From Luther's "Our Father, Thou in Heav'n Above" ("Vater unser im Himmelreich") included in Robin Leaver's *Catherine Winkworth: The Influence of Her Translations on English Hymnody* (St. Louis: Concordia Publishing House, 1978), 155-156.

[143] Watson, 206.

live one day at a time, and not to worry and be anxious about the distant and the unknown future."[144] Agur, the author of the sayings in Proverbs 30, expressed what is the message of the fourth petition.

> ...give me neither poverty nor riches, but give me only my daily bread. Otherwise, I may have too much and disown you and say, 'Who is the Lord?' Or I may become poor and steal and so dishonor the name of my God (Prov. 30:8-9).

---

[144] Barclay, *The Gospel of Matthew* Vol. 2, 326.

Chapter Thirteen

Seeking Forgiveness of Sins

Petition Five, Part One

There is a wonderful book of a year's worth of daily devotions written by Joni Eeareckson Tada. For her February 27 entry in *Diamonds in the Dust* she offered the following entitled "Forgiven and Forgotten Sins." She wrote:

> Somewhere in the back of my memory, I have a list. It's called "Forgiven Sins I Can't Forget." This list isn't long, but it contains a handful of personal transgressions that, in my estimation, tend toward the vile and disgusting. In my lower moments, these old sins flash in neon lights in front of my thinking. I cringe, recalling those awful things I am capable of doing. Against my own conscience, I am unable to stand. Thankfully, my conscience does not render the final judgment. Christ does. And, oh, how I praise the Lord that He keeps no lists. To be sure, He takes notice of every sin. But does He keep account? No. For one thing, God is love and 1 Corinthians 13 says that love "keeps no record of wrongs." For another thing, Psalm 103:12 reminds us that "as far as the east is from the west, so far has he removed our transgressions from us." When we confess our sin, we acknowledge that Christ paid the penalty for it on the cross. He wipes the slate clean. He washes away the guilt and cleans our conscience. In other words, He erases the list. When it comes to the sin of His truly repentant children, God forgives and forgets. That's the nature of His grace.[145]

---

[145] Joni Eeareckson Tada. *Diamonds in the Dust: 366 Sparkling Devotions* (Grand Rapids: Zondervan, 1993).

The subjects of repentance and forgiveness of sins are spoken to in the fifth petition of the Lord's Prayer. Most versions of the petition use the term *debts*, as in the NIV which reads: "Forgive us our debts as we also have forgiven our debtors." Why, we may ask, did Jesus use a *financial* term to refer to *sins*? Why did he teach his disciples to seek forgiveness of sins? Why did he include in this petition the clause "as we also have forgiven our debtors?" And why did he, after the body of the prayer, offer added commentary? "For if you forgive [others] when they sin against you, your heavenly Father will forgive you. But if you do not forgive [others] their sins, your Father will not forgive yours sins" (Mt. 6:14-15). In the KJV the petition reads: "And forgive us our *debts*, as we forgive our *debtors*." Luke's account says: "And forgive us our *sins*; for we also forgive everyone that is *indebted* to us." Jesus' added commentary in the KJV reads: "For if ye forgive [others] their *trespasses* your heavenly Father will also forgive you; but if ye forgive not [others] their *trespasses*, neither will your Father forgive your *trespasses*." We've discovered three English words, *debts*, *sins*, and *trespasses*, related to Jesus' teaching. We may ask: why are three terms used? And why, if *trespasses* is not the term used within the body of the prayer in either account, do some Christian communities use it in their praying of the prayer? We will need to address each of these matters.

This chapter is the first of two based on this petition and the added commentary. Although it is not possible to separate completely the thoughts in the petition which speak of God's forgiving us and our forgiving others, yet because the phrases are so full of important spiritual truth, we shall divide our examination into two parts. Here we will focus on an understanding of the meanings of the terms used for sin, then consider the several components of repentance, which is the requirement for God's granting forgiveness.

Understanding the Terms

The reason why there are three English terms for sin is because there are three different New Testament Greek terms. Within the body of the prayer in Matthew's account, the term is *opheilemata*. This is actually one of five Greek terms translated *sin* found in the New Testament.

Each of the five terms has a particular shade of meaning. One or another of them was used in a particular passage depending on the specific meaning desired. The best rendering of *opheilemata* in Matthew is *debts*. It is the translation found in many versions of the Bible (KJV, NKJV, NIV, NASB, RSV, NRSV, ESV). *Opheilemata* refers to the spiritual debt we owe God because of the owing of our very existence to God; and more specifically as far as the Lord's Prayer is concerned, because we are in spiritual debt to God due to our sin. Sin is pictured as a debt. Sinners are pictured as debtors. Therefore sin is viewed as a wrong and as a wrong which must be righted in some way. Either debtors must pay the debts, or they will receive punishment, or possibly the debtor may be pardoned. In some way the one to whom we owe the debt must be satisfied. There must be a resolution to the problem of our spiritual debt to God. The term, therefore, is a metaphor likening our sin to that of a financial debt. Amplifying the financial imagery Barth remarked: "...we are in default in our relation to God, in what we owe him. We have a debt due him, and if we cannot pay it, we remain in default."[146] He continued: "We are God's debtors. We owe him not something, whether it be little or much, but, quite simply, our person in its totality; we owe him ourselves, since we are his creatures, sustained and nourished by his goodness."[147]

Of course, there is *no possibility* of our being able to escape the debt we owe God; and the message of the scriptures is that we could never do enough good deeds to offset or satisfy the debt. Either we pay with our lives and suffer the condemnation of God, or we may receive a pardon. Thankfully, God, in his mercy, offered in the death of Christ to pay the debt. He cancels the debt, pardoning, or rather acquitting all who sincerely acknowledge Jesus as their debt payer, their Savior and Lord.

In Jesus' commentary which follows the body of the prayer in Matthew's account, the Greek term for sin is *paraptomata*. Literally, it means *slipping across a line*, and is appropriately translated trespass,

---

[146] Barth, *Prayer*, 74.

[147] Ibid.

transgression, or violation. Whereas a fourth term for sin, *parabasis* (e.g. Rom. 4:15), conveys the idea of *deliberately* stepping across a line, a deliberate violation of proper God-intended behavior, and whereas a fifth term *anomia* (e.g. 1 Jn. 3:4) means lawlessness, *paraptomata* may refer more to *unintentional* mistakes, sins none the less, but unintentional. The point Jesus may have been making by adding these remarks, this added warning, is that whether sin is intentional or unintentional, it is still sin. Even unintentional sins make us debtors to God; and God's pardon must include cancellation of any kind of trespass, transgression, or violation. Moreover, should others violate us, whether intentionally or unintentionally, we are to forgive them as freely and as sincerely and completely as God forgives us.

In Luke's account (11:4) the term *hamartias* is used in the first half of the petition: "and forgive us our sins." *Hamartias* literally means *missing a target*, as in archery. It conveys the idea of *falling short*, not quite being on line, a failure to be what we should be. As we can see, this term provides another shade of meaning for sin. In most versions of the Bible, *hamartias* in Luke's report of Jesus' prayer is translated sins. In the second half of the petition we read in the KJV: "for we also forgive everyone that is indebted to us." There *opheilonti* is used.

The three terms used by Matthew and Luke, *opheilemata, paraptomata*, and *hamartias*, while conveying different shades of meaning, all refer to sin. The message is clear, and it is a central theme of the scriptures. We humans are sinners. We are in debt to God because of our sin and in need of forgiveness. Not only so, the petition and the added commentary make it clear that no matter how sins may be thought of, they are still sin. Moreover, in the second part of the petition and in the added warning Jesus taught there is a *relationship* between our forgiving others and God forgiving us as Christians, a relationship we will examine. It seems that in addition to there being two parts to this petition, there must be two categories of forgiveness; the forgiveness of God *when* entering the kingdom of God's grace, when we first make our expression of trust in Christ; and the forgiveness of God *after* entering the kingdom of God's grace. This is important to distinguish because the thrust of Jesus' use of forgiveness in the Lord's Prayer is after entering the kingdom; the reason being, the prayer was taught to disciples, his declared followers. Making this distinction will be helpful for interpreting and explaining the significance of the second half of the petition and the added remarks.

Nevertheless, the subject of the forgiveness of sins *when* entering the kingdom is not outside our present interest. We will examine God's forgiveness *when* and *after* entering the kingdom, not that the *nature* of God's forgiveness changes in any way, but that the *terms* of God's forgiving seem to be unique in each instance. Making the distinction between being acquitted at initial entrance, and being forgiven after we've entered and begun to increase in the kingdom of God's grace is important for a complete appreciation of what forgiveness means in the New Testament and in the Lord's Prayer in particular.

Repenting of Sins

Evidently Jesus referred to sins as debts and sinners as debtors to underscore the seriousness of our human predicament. We need to ask God to forgive us, to acquit us because we are sinners, because we owe God a debt for having committed wrongs against him, against his holy standard of human behavior; and because when we sin we mar the image of God it has been intended for us to reflect. Even if we've never committed what may be called the more serious acts (e.g. adultery, murder), our thinking and motivations, our dispositions are out of line. They miss the mark. The problem is the condition of the human heart.

Following the resurrection, Jesus opened the minds of the disciples and said to them: "This is what is written: the Christ will suffer and rise from the dead on the third day, and repentance and forgiveness of sins will be preached in his name to all nations..."(Lk. 24:47). *Repentance* and *forgiveness* go together. There can be no forgiveness unless there is repentance. Repentance was repeatedly called for by prophets, by Jesus, and by the apostles. For example, the word of the Lord came to unfaithful Judah through Jeremiah: "If you repent, I will restore you..." (Jer. 15:19).

Jesus' cousin, John the Baptist, came preaching in the desert saying: "Repent, for the kingdom of heaven is near" (Mt. 3:1-2). When Jesus began his public ministry he preached the same message (Mt. 4:17). Jesus sent out his disciples two by two. "They went out and preached that people should repent" (Mk. 6:12). After Jesus' ascension and the disciples' anointing by the Holy Spirit, the apostle Peter delivered a stirring message.

> 'Repent and be baptized, everyone of you, in the name of Jesus Christ for the forgiveness of your sins. And you will receive the gift of the Holy Spirit...' those who accepted his message were baptized, and about three thousand were added to their number that day (Acts 2:38-41).

So how may we understand repentance? There are *four main ingredients* to true repentance before forgiveness will be conferred. They include *comprehension, contrition, confession*, and *conversion*.[148]

Comprehension. For many people it may be that they truly do not understand that all persons are sinners, that they as individuals are considered sinful by God, that they have been sinful since birth (Ps. 51:5) and are in need of spiritual restoration. They may have no awareness of what God's inspired Word teaches. For example, John wrote: "If we claim to be without sin we deceive ourselves," (1 Jn.1:8). "If we claim we have not sinned, we make [God] out to be a liar" (1 Jn. 1:10), because through his Spirit he inspired certain persons to compose the sacred writings we have as our Bible, and in those pages we read over and over again that human beings are sinners, "all have sinned and fall short of the glory of God" (Rom. 3:23). Everyone is a debtor to God. In the eternal bank account we have insufficient funds. We're bankrupt! We're in default in our relationship with God. We are in arrears with God and deserve the enforcement of the law of God upon us. "There is no one righteous, not even one" (Rom. 3:10). Our iniquities have separated us from God (Isa. 59:2), and the wages of our sins is spiritual death (Rom. 6:23), the state of eternal separation from God. Human beings must come to the place where they understand the seri-

---

[148] Adapted from Watson, 217-219.

Seeking Forgiveness of Sins

ousness of their sin condition and realize that only God can save them from the consequences of their sin.

Pardon for sin thankfully is the core message of Christianity. The wages of sin is surely death, "but the gift of God is eternal life in Christ Jesus our Lord" (Rom. 6:23). By faith in Christ the condemnation which we deserve is removed.[149] "Salvation is found in no one else, for there is no other name under heaven given to [us] by which we must be saved" (Acts 4:12). Jesus paid the debt we owe with his sinless life offered as an atoning sacrifice. So complete was the payment that Jesus, when breathing his last on the cross used another financial term as he declared: "It is finished" (Jn. 19:30). Finished (*tetelestai*) was a term used to announce a final installment, an ultimate payment.[150] The first step toward true repentance is *comprehending* the biblical teaching regarding sin.

Contrition. The second component of repentance is *contrition*, which means a brokenness of heart, a rending of the heart, as in Isaiah 65:14. "My servants will sing out of the joy of their heart, but you will cry out from anguish of heart and wail in brokenness of spirit." We must be truly sorry for our sins. In biblical days such sincerity was expressed by beating one's chest (e.g. Lk. 18:13), by tearing one's clothes or even plucking out some of one's hair (Ezra 9:3). There must be inner, heartfelt contrition.

Confession. Then there must be *confession*, in the sense of admitting one's sins. "Against you, you only, have I sinned," confessed David, "and done what is evil in your sight" (Ps. 51:4). Confession is a venting, an expression of one's true sorrow. Needless to say, both contrition and confession are needed. There's something about admitting one's sin which shows that one's sorrow is genuine. On the other hand, merely saying we're sorry without heartfelt sorrow is not genuine confession. Both are needed.

Conversion. True repentance is not complete, however, without *conversion*, which means a *turning from sin* and a *turning toward God* (e.g.

---

[149] *Calvin's Commentaries* Vol. XVI, 327.

[150] Lucado, 114.

Jud. 10:15-16). We must *understand* (comprehension) that there is a need for repentance; we must be *sorrowful* for our sin (contrition); we must *express* that sorrow (confession); and then we must intentionally *turn* (conversion) from our sin, turn to and seek to be faithful and follow the ways of God.

In the New Testament the verb *convert* (*strepho*) means to turn, to turn around, or turn toward. It is a metaphorical term for changing one's spiritual direction. It refers to the turning of a soul from sin toward God. We may even think of conversion as returning to God. Just as in a change of direction when driving a car there is an initial turn and then a proceeding in the new direction, so also in spiritual conversion there needs to be both an initial turn to God, then a continuation in the direction one has turned. Conversion, therefore, is both an initial action of the will to turn from one direction to another, and then it is a process of continuing and proceeding in the new direction. Whereas previously we introduced the idea that there is a distinction between God's forgiveness when we come to faith in Christ, and God's forgiveness after we make a decision to be a disciple of Jesus, so also we must be perfectly clear that when we speak of conversion, or someone being converted, we need to remember there are two aspects to conversion; the initial turn, and then the proceeding in the new direction until the ultimate destination is reached. After making the initial turn, there is a lifelong process in which, hopefully, there will take place a gradual transformation of character (e.g. Rom. 12:2, 2 Cor. 3:18), a process called *sanctification*.

Having said that, it is not unusual to hear people speak of *being converted, being saved, making a profession of faith,* or *receiving Jesus Christ,* all of which are biblically based expressions, meaning becoming Christian in the sense of making the initial turn from sins' ways to God's ways. In Acts 15:3, for example, we read: "The church [at Antioch] sent [Paul and Barnabas] on their way, and as they traveled through Phoenicia and Samaria, they told how the Gentiles had been converted," meaning how they had made the initial turn, how they had made a change of direction in their lives, how they chose to turn from the direction of sin to the direction of Jesus Christ.

Seeking Forgiveness of Sins

Regarding conversion in terms of the initial turn, we may ask: what are the terms whereby God's gift of forgiveness is granted, and by which we are justified to enter the kingdom of God's grace? As with any gift, there is a giver and a receiver. God is the giver; we are the potential receivers. Salvation is the gift of God which must be received in order for the acquittal to be conferred. No one else can receive the gift for us. Each one of us must receive the gift individually. Being baptized or being a member of a church does not necessarily mean that one has received the gift. It was Billy Graham who said: "Just because you are born in a garage, that doesn't make you a car."[151] Each one of us must ask in order to receive, or we must accept the offer extended.

Another conceptualization which the Bible provides, a picture of the response required by us to God's offer of forgiveness, is that given in Revelation 3:20; it is a picture of opening a door. Jesus said: "Here I am! I stand at the door and knock. If anyone hears my voice and opens the door, I will come in and eat with him, and he with me." In order for forgiveness, pictured as the fellowship setting, to be realized, we must respond to the knock and open the door. Accepting a gift and opening a door are figurative descriptions of what we must do to make the initial turn. In the terms of which we've spoken above, people must come to the place where they understand their need for repentance, they must be truly sorry for their sins, then confess them, and then be converted by inviting, receiving and welcoming the Spirit of Jesus Christ into their hearts.

My initial turn took place in 1962 at an evangelistic meeting led by Jack Wyrtzen of Word of Life camp, Schroon Lake, New York. Many people over the past fifty years have responded to Billy Graham's invitation at one of his crusades. Some persons make the turn in the quietness of a home where one leads another to pray and commit his or her life to Christ. It is our responsibility to explain the offer of forgiveness and help lead others to make the turn, because no matter what the circumstances, all people have the same need; we're all sinners in debt to

---

[151] Quoted in Robert Backhouse, comp. *1500 Illustrations for Preaching and Teaching* (London: Marshall Pickering, 1991), 183.

God; we are in need of forgiveness; we are in need of God's pardon. The initial turn must take place in order for God's forgiveness of sins to be realized in our lives, and in order for us to be endowed and anointed by the Holy Spirit who prompts and enables us to make the turn in the first place, and who assists us subsequently in our growth in Christ. All who receive Christ, all who believe in his name, are justified to be forgiven children of God, members of the kingdom family (Jn. 1:12). If we confess with our mouths, "Jesus is Lord," and believe in our hearts that God raised him from the dead, we will be acquitted (Rom. 10:9). Our sins will be *dismissed, sent away,* as the term *forgiven* (*aphiemi*) literally suggests,[152] imagery drawn from the Israelite observance of the Day of Atonement (e.g. Lev. 16 and 23:26-32) in which the scapegoat bore the sins of the people and was sent away alive into the wilderness to die. As with the scapegoat, Jesus became the substitute victim for sinners. Someone may ask: Would a loving God condemn unbelievers to an eternal destiny as hell is pictured in the scriptures? The answer is a sobering yes, because they have not accepted God's terms of pardon; and, as Jesus explained, actually they condemn themselves (Jn. 3:18). Receiving Christ, acknowledging him as our debt payer, is absolutely necessary for forgiveness to be granted.

    This is the forgiveness of God *when* persons initially enter the kingdom of God's grace. Understanding this will help us grasp the primary thrust of Jesus' intention in this petition to which we will direct our attention in the next chapter. Those who have yet to surrender their lives to God, are encouraged to repent of their sins and invite the Spirit of Jesus Christ into their lives. There's no getting around it unless one is ready to accept the consequences for lack of surrender. Who in his or her right mind would want to neglect so great a salvation? In the words of the apostle Paul (2 Cor. 7:10): "Godly sorrow brings repentance that leads to salvation and leaves no regret."

---

[152] Vine, 452.

Seeking Forgiveness of Sins

Merciful and loving God, speak to the heart which needs to surrender. Draw to yourself those who have yet to receive the Spirit of Jesus into their hearts. Help them truly to be sorry for their sins, to admit their sinfulness, to invite Christ into their lives, and to intentionally turn from sin and turn toward you and your ways. We pray through Jesus Christ, the Savior of our souls and the Lord of our lives, who taught his disciples to pray, saying: "Our Father...."

Chapter Fourteen

Forgiving Others

Petition Five, Part Two

In the February 15th entry of the 2001 *Our Daily Bread* devotional guide, there was a poignant story of a man inwardly convicted of a broken relationship with his brother. The account read:

> How far would you travel to put things right with a brother who hadn't spoken to you in ten years? Would you go 300 miles from Iowa to Wisconsin? On a riding lawn mower? Unable to drive a car and despising bus travel, Alvin Straight... a 73-year old-man...decided it was time to end the silence, stop the hating, and break down the wall of anger he and his brother had built between them.[153]

The devotional writer noted the words of Jesus: "If you bring your gift to the altar, and remember that your brother has something against you, leave your gift there before the altar, and go your way. First be reconciled to your brother, and then come and offer your gift" (Matt. 5:23-24). A similar principle is given in the fifth petition of the Lord's Prayer. We have the privilege of seeking God's forgiveness for our sins. However, as we will explore presently, we may do so *so long* as we have forgiven the sins of those who may have wronged us.

In the last chapter we introduced the petition by discussing the meanings of the terms for sin given in the two biblical versions of the prayer and in Jesus' added commentary (Mt. 6:14-15). We also examined four components of repentance: understanding that all persons are sinners (comprehension); being truly sorry for our sins (contrition); admitting our sins to God (confession); and intentionally turning from

---

[153] From *Our Daily Bread* (February 15, 2001) Vol. 45, No. 11. Grand Rapids: RBC Ministries, 2000.

our sins and turning toward God (conversion). Full repentance is the requirement for God's forgiving our sins *when* we make the initial turn and receive the Spirit of Jesus Christ into our lives, thus entering the kingdom of God's grace.

The petition, as well as the prayer as a whole, assumes that the persons praying are already believers, for the prayer was taught to disciples. The *main focus* of the petition, therefore, is God's forgiveness *after* persons have entered the kingdom of God's grace. We've asked previously why did Jesus include the phrase "as we also have forgiven our debtors," and why, after the body of the prayer did he provide additional commentary on this particular petition? Moreover, why should we forgive others who wrong us intentionally or unintentionally? Does Jesus place a *condition* on God's forgiveness?

Understanding the Condition

In answering the last question we have to be very careful. If we were to think that God would not forgive our sins upon entrance into his kingdom unless we had already forgiven others their sins, then we would be mistaken and incorrect in our interpretation, because, as the Bible teaches, it is only by God's grace that we are pardoned, through repentance and faith (Eph. 2:8-9). However, *after* we enter the kingdom and it is expected that we begin to increase in the kingdom and do God's will, *then* it would be hypocritical of us to pray for continued, ongoing, daily forgiveness if we had not forgiven any others who may have wronged us, particularly if they asked to be forgiven. As a Christian it is an offense to God to withhold forgiveness of wrongs committed by others when God had already forgiven our sins. It is a slap in the face of God. Indeed, not to forgive others may indicate possibly that we may not have been genuinely sorry for our own sins; and if that is the case, it is possible that we may not have entered God's kingdom. A sobering thought. One is intended evidently to be a sign of the other. The petition and the added commentary indicate that after we've received God's pardon by faith in Christ and entered the kingdom, there is a *condition* attached to God's on-going forgiveness of our sins.

Repentance is still the primary mode of requesting and receiving pardon. We should repent and turn everyday to be in fellowship with God. "We sin daily," explained Watson, "and must ask for daily pardon as well as for daily bread. Besides, a Christian's pardon is not so sure but he may desire to have a clearer evidence of it...A full absolution from all sin is not pronounced till the day of judgment (Acts 3:19)."[154] However, the *condition* of God's conferring on-going forgiveness is our forgiveness of others; and that is the primary reason for the inclusion of the second phrase in the petition. Barclay said: "Human forgiveness and divine forgiveness are inextricably inter-combined. Forgiveness of our fellowman and God's forgiveness of us cannot be separated; they are interlinked and interdependent."[155]

Jesus emphasized the importance of this matter by repeating it and issuing a warning to disciples in his added commentary. As a Christian it is a serious matter not to forgive others. Interpreting the warning, Frank Stagg commented that forgiving others helps believers to be fit for receiving forgiveness. "It is not that God is unwilling to forgive the unforgiving but that the condition of the unforgiving is such that they are incapable of receiving forgiveness. When the door is closed, it is closed from both sides. What blocks the flow of mercy or forgiveness from us blocks its flow to us (see Mt. 18:21-35)."[156] In addition, as Calvin pointed out, when we have not forgiven others we are, in fact, asking God not to forgive us![157]

A further word of caution and explanation is in order regarding the word "as" in the petition. The petition does not mean "forgive us our debts because we have forgiven our debtors," or "forgive us our debts since we have forgiven our debtors." Both would come closer to a works-righteousness theology. G. Campbell Morgan (1863-1945), a British Congregationalist preacher, commented: "God never does business on the basis of a promissory note."[158] What it does say and mean

---

[154] Watson, 222.

[155] Barclay, *The Gospel of Matthew* Vol. 222.

[156] Stagg, 116.

[157] *Institutes* III, XX, 45.

[158] Morgan, 84.

is "forgive us our debts as," meaning *in the same way as,* or *in the same manner as* "we also have forgiven our debtors." The clause "commits the pray-er to actions which back up the petition just offered."[159] In other words, we pray the petition as we do in order to put ourselves in a proper posture for requesting forgiveness for our own sins. In so doing we demonstrate we are truly grateful for God's forgiveness, and that we are willing to accept the responsibility of being faithful witnesses of God's forgiving nature. *As* is a similitude, meaning that we are admonished to imitate God in forgiving. The tense of the verb (past, aorist) literally indicates "as we also have forgiven our debtors."[160] The petition means: forgive us our sins in proportion to how we forgive others. G. Campbell Morgan concluded: "We must get our forgiving done before we can ask for forgiveness."[161]

Let us return to the questions raised previously. Why did Jesus include the phrase "as we also have forgiven our debtors"? The answer is to help us realize we may seek forgiveness of sins, indeed we must because we are debtors, but only as we have forgiven others. Why did Jesus provide added commentary on this petition? The answer is to emphasize the importance of forgiving others. God will refuse to forgive Christians their on-going sins unless they forgive others who may have wronged them.

Reasons for Forgiving

Why should we forgive others? We shall offer nine reasons. First, forgiving others is not an option. God commands us to forgive. "And when you stand praying, if you hold anything against anyone, forgive him, so that your Father in heaven may forgive yours sins" (Mk. 11:25; see also Lk. 17:3-4, Eph. 4:32, Col. 3:13).

---

[159] N. T. Wright. *The Lord and His Prayer* (Grand Rapids: Wm. B. Eerdmans Publishing Company, 1996), 54.

[160] Marvin R. Vincent. *Vincent's Word Studies of the New Testament Vol. I* (Peabody, Mass: Hendrickson Publishers, n.d., originally published in 1886), 43.

[161] Morgan, 84.

Second, we are to forgive because we have been given the responsibility as Christ's ambassadors to mirror the image of God, to reflect his character as a way of making God known in the world (Ex. 34:6-7). Moreover, Jesus forgave sins, even as he hung on the cross (Lk. 23:34). To make Christ known, we must forgive (2 Cor. 3:16, 18). Helmut Thielicke (1908-1986), outstanding German preacher during the Nazi regime, said in a sermon on the Lord's Prayer.

> ...forgiveness provides the sole possibility of the world's ever escaping the law of the echo, that dreadful, chaotic law by which nations and individuals are constantly inflaming and provoking one another because of the 'other's fault', and swelling the avalanche of guilt and retribution to even more gigantic proportions.
>
> We are always echoes. The only question is: echoes of what? Either we are echoes of the injustice, the intrigue, the chicanery, the meanness that is around us, and then we ourselves become scheming, cheating, and mean. Or we are echoes of Jesus Christ and therefore echoes of that forgiving, renewing, creative love that comes to us from the Father. Then we ourselves become loving, renewing, forgiving, creative, and positive.[162]

Our Christian lives are intended to be echoes, mirror images of the forgiveness of God in Christ, thus making him known. Our forgiveness of others, therefore, becomes an experiential sign to them of God's willingness to forgive. Only by mirroring God's forgiveness will others have a chance of conceptualizing God's offer of pardon for spiritual debts.

Third, and not unrelated to the second, forgiving others is a sign to us, it is *evidence, proof*[163] that we have been forgiven by God. Forgiving others is the most vivid way God has provided to give us *assurance* of his

---

[162] Helmut Thielicke. *Our Heavenly Father: Sermons in the Lord's Prayer* trans. by John W. Doberstein (New York: Harper & Row, Publishers, 1960), 113.

[163] D. Martyn Lloyd-Jones. *Studies in the Sermon on the Mount*, Vol. Two (Grand Rapids: Wm. B. Eerdmans Publishing Company, 1996), 75.

pardon, "a sign alongside the promise in Luke 6:37..."[164] Forgiving others pictures, proves, and convinces us that God can and will forgive sins.

Fourth, as we have said above, forgiving others demonstrates the sincerity of our contrition and confession and places us in a favorable position to receive on-going forgiveness of sins. Forgiving others is a test of our sincerity. "Be on guard then," taught Cyril of Jerusalem (c. 315-386), "lest because of the small and light offenses committed against you, you block God's forgiveness for very serious sins."[165] "Sin can hinder the bounty of God," declared John Wesley.[166] We should forgive others because after we enter the kingdom, the *works* we do, including forgiving others, become especially important and are the appropriate expression of our faith. We are to "produce fruit in keeping with repentance" (Mt. 3:8). "Faith without deeds is dead" (Jas. 2:26). Our works are the proof of our faith, evidence to ourselves and to others. We should be doers of the word and not hearers only (Jas. 1:22). As Christians we are expected to work out our salvation (Phil. 2:12), to make our calling and election sure (2 Pet. 1:10). As we have received Christ Jesus as Lord, we are to continue to live in him (Col. 2:6). In other words, in order to increase and persevere in the kingdom, we must do good works, not the least of which is forgiving others. We are expected to uphold our part of the bargain, so to speak. It is vital to our spiritual health and witness. We will let Watson's words conclude this point.

> ...[Christ] had the special purpose of making mutual love a Christian obligation, and the continued forgiveness of the neighbor the primary and foremost duty of Christians, second only to faith and the reception of forgiveness.[167]

> ...the forgiveness of sins takes place in two ways: first inwardly,

---

[164] Janzow, 93.

[165] Cyril of Jerusalem, XXIII, 16.

[166] Wesley, 339.

[167] Watson, 149.

Forgiving Others

through the Gospel and the Word of God, which is received by faith in the heart toward God; second, outwardly through works...(2 Pet. 1:10).[168]

...why Christ attached this addition to the prayer. He did so to establish the closest possible bonds between us and to preserve His Christendom in the unity of the Spirit (Eph. 4:3), both in faith and love. We must not let any sin or fault divide us or rob us of our faith and of everything else.[169]

Fifth, we should forgive others because we would want to be forgiven by others as well. As the Golden Rule puts it: "So in everything do to others what you would have them do to you, for this sums up the Law and the Prophets" (Mt. 7:12). In Victor Hugo's novel *Les Miserables*, Jean Valjean served a nineteen year sentence for stealing a loaf of bread in order to feed his sister's family. Eventually he was set free. A Bishop was the only one who befriended the embittered man. Valjean rewarded him by stealing some of his silver. He was caught red-handed by the police. The Bishop was then called to the police station to charge Valjean formally. However, instead he brought Valjean his candlestick holders as well. Valjean became forever changed. He extended grace to an orphan and raised her as his own. He forgave the policeman who wanted to put him back in jail. When he died, he was holding in his hand the two candlesticks that the Bishop gave him. What changed him? He learned to extend mercy, because mercy had been extended to him.[170]

Sixth, we should forgive others to guard against hurting ourselves. People who have an unforgiving spirit often are prone to illness, such as ulcers, because they have no peace within (Isa. 57:20-21). "Nothing but forgiveness," wrote Watson, "can give ease to a troubled conscience."[171]

---

[168] Ibid.

[169] Ibid., 154.

[170] Anecdote given in *SermonIllustrations.com* for September 12, 1999.

[171] Watson, 227.

Seventh, we should forgive others so as not to hurt them. Not to forgive may result in them not forgiving still others. By not forgiving others we may be starting a chain reaction, contributing to the harm of many people. "Make every effort to live in peace with all [people] and to be holy; without holiness no one will see the Lord. See to it that no one misses the grace of God and that no bitter root grows up to cause trouble and defile many" (Heb. 12:14-15).

Eighth, we should forgive others because forgiving restores relationships; and within the Body of Christ in particular we are admonished to do all we can to live harmoniously with one another (Rom. 12:18, 1 Th. 5:13, Heb. 12:14). We've been given the ministry of reconciliation (2 Cor. 5:18). It is a part of our witness. We are commanded to be peacemakers.[172] Luther's chorale text makes the point.

> Forgive our sins, that they no more
> May grieve and haunt us as before,
> As we forgive their trespasses
> Who unto us have done amiss;
> Thus let us dwell in charity,
> And serve each other willingly.[173]

Ninth, we should forgive others because not to do so undermines the Gospel. Failing to forgive sends a signal that Christianity is not all that it is cracked up to be. Our forgiveness of one another in the Christian community and of others outside as well, speaks loudly of the integrity of the Gospel. By such a virtue will others know that we are Christ's disciples (Jn. 13:35). Ours should be the prayer of Charles Wesley.

> Our trespasses forgive;
> And when absolved we live,

---

[172] Cyprian. "On the Lord's Prayer" (Treatise IV), *Ante-Nicene Fathers* Vol. 5, 454 (paragraph 23).

[173] Stanza 6 of Luther's Chorale text "Our Father, Thou in Heav'n Above."

Thou our life of grace maintain;
Lest we from God depart,
Lose thy pardoning love again,
Grant us a forgiving heart.[174]

The point is clear, as Christians forgiving others is expected by God. A comment by the famous evangelist Dwight L. Moody (1837-1899) underscores one of the significances of the petition. "I firmly believe," he said, "a great many prayers are not answered because we are not willing to forgive someone."[175] The petition moves us to examine our hearts. It helps us be honest about ourselves and our relationships. May God enable each one of us to be reconciled to anyone by whom we may have been wronged, or for whom we have withheld our full acceptance or forgiveness. *Our Father in heaven, please forgive us our sins in the same way we have forgiven those who have sinned against us.*

Liturgical Usage

To conclude the discussion of the fifth petition, the following is offered as an answer to the question raised previously. Why, if *trespasses* is not the term used within the body of the Lord's Prayer in either account, do some Christian communities use it in their praying of the prayer? The answer is fairly simple and it is historical in nature.

The English scholar William Tyndale (c.1490-1536) translated from the original languages much of the Bible into English. He was the first person known to do so. Because of this accomplishment he has been called the "Father of the English Bible." Much of his work is that which was retained as the KJV. In his original translation Tyndale introduced the term *trespasses* in the body of the Lord's Prayer, and it has been used ever since, particularly for its historical significance, most notably by Anglicans, Episcopalians, and Methodists.[176] It became the *official*

---

[174] G. Osborn. *The Poetical Works of John and Charles Wesley*, Vol. X (London: Wesleyan-Methodist Conference Office, 1871), 178-179.

[175] Quote of Dwight L. Moody given in *The One Year Book of Personal Prayer* (February 22nd inclusion). Wheaton, IL: Tyndale House Publishers, 1991.

[176] Ayo, 23 & 72.

liturgical language usage for *The Book of Common Prayer* (1662) even though in the KJV of 1611 Tyndale's translation was changed more appropriately to *debts*. Evidently the use of *trespasses* in the Church of England was so well-known and engrained in peoples' minds before the issuing of the KJV, that those who formulated *The Book of Common Prayer* felt it would be too difficult to change the practice. Historical and liturgical factors, therefore, are behind the use of *trespasses* by many Christian communities.

Some Christian communities use *sins* in the praying of the prayer. Two reasons for this are because of its *comprehensiveness* and what seems to be the *contemporary need*. Since there are three English terms (debts, trespasses, and sins) which have been associated with the prayer, since there are two biblical sources from which we may draw (Matt. 6:9-15, Lk 11:1-4), and since the usage of the prayer is largely in public worship where we should do all we can to communicate the intention of scripture as clearly, as fully, and as faithfully as possible, *sins*, as it is generally understood, takes into consideration all of the shades of meaning of the three Greek terms associated with the prayer: being indebted to God, unintentionally slipping across the line of correct behavior (trespasses), and definitely missing the mark of God's standards (sins). *Sins* is comprehensive, it includes all three descriptions of our sinful situation. Using *debts* is perfectly proper if one uses the Matthew version. Using *sins* is appropriate if anyone were to use the Luke account or formulate a liturgical rendering drawn both from Matthew and Luke. *Trespasses*, it would seem, is not appropriate because it is not the term given within Jesus' prayer in either account, and it's meaning may refer more to the *un*intentional sins. It is not comprehensive enough. It gives an incomplete message. *Sins*, as we use the term generally, is comprehensive. It encompasses all of the above meanings.

Regarding the contemporary need, it may be that most people think of themselves more highly than they should. That is not to say most people think of themselves as superior to others; or that we should think of ourselves as inferior to others; but rather we like to think we're really not that bad, or as bad as someone else; and, therefore, words like *debts* and *trespasses* soften the concept of our being sinners. The scriptures make it clear that all people sin and fall short, as with *hamartias*, definitely significantly short of the glory of God (Rom. 3:23). We are all sinners. There's no getting out of it or denying it. Right from the start we are sinners (Psalm 51:1-12). In our present cultural setting, where the philosophy of personal preference dominates peoples' view of living, where people seem less inclined to behave according to any standard of conduct, where fewer and fewer people it seems feel shame for wrongful behavior, it is important for Christians to uphold God's view of the human situation; to hold up before themselves and their neighbors the truth of our spiritual condition under God. We do not only occasionally commit some minor infraction of God's pattern for human thinking or conduct, although some people are more or less prone to do so. All of us are violators in one way or another. We do not simply trespass the line of right and wrong once in a great while and only unintentionally. We are in debt to God because of our sin. We miss the target. The term *sins*, as generally spoken in our culture, more comprehensively includes all shades of meaning of the terms for sin in the New Testament. *Debts* may not be understood fully by many who pray the Lord's Prayer unless it is explained. *Sins*, it seems to me, is preferred, in that it hits the subject right on the head. It tells us we've done wrong, intentionally or unintentionally; we're in debt to God; we're missing the mark of the God-given standard of behavior. It says to us we must own up to our sins, our transgressions, trespasses, spiritual debts to God and others, our wrongs, our failings. It tells us we need forgiveness, just as others need forgiveness from God and from us. Over time the meanings of words can change somewhat. We need to use the best language of the day which faithfully renders the original. *Debts* is very appropriate. *Sins*, used in the NLT throughout the petition and the added commentary, really accomplishes the task in today's culture.

Chapter Fifteen
Praying for Leniency
Petition Six, Part One

Stanza two of "What a Friend We Have in Jesus" asks:

> Have we trials and temptations?
> Is there trouble anywhere?
> We should never be discouraged,
> Take it to the Lord in prayer.
> Can we find a friend so faithful
> Who will all our sorrows share?
> Jesus knows our every weakness,
> Take it to the Lord in prayer.

This well-known hymn text points out that even as Christians we are frail. Our lives include trials, temptations and sorrows. We are prone to being discouraged. We need help! The admonishment is given to take our circumstances to God in prayer, for Jesus cares, he knows our frame, and he intercedes for us even now (Heb. 7:25).

The last petition of the Lord's Prayer assumes our weakness, our need for strength under trial and resistance against temptations and the Evil One. As we discuss the sixth petition, it will be helpful to think of it as one request with two parts, and thus we will need to devote two chapters to it. It is similar in literary form with that of Hebrew poetry. "Lead us not into temptation" is parallel with "but deliver us from evil." Both clauses deal with the subject of God's *protection*. Although not entirely the same in meaning, *temptation* and *evil* are related concerns, and, therefore, linked together. Our first concern will be to define the term translated *temptation*. This will help us understand why the first half of the petition is a prayer for leniency.

Defining Temptation

Sometimes the language which has come down to us had meanings in a former era which are not the connotations we associate with certain terms today, or our understanding of a New Testament term is more complete than in days past. Consequently, when people read some words in the scriptures they may get the wrong idea regarding their usage. When considering *lead us not into temptation*, one may think the phrase means: "Please God, don't try to make me sin." While there may be an element of this meaning in the phrase, its true emphasis is not that at all. The Greek term (*peirasmos*) does not mean solicitation to evil; it does not mean seduction by God, tempting us or making us sin and fall. This is not what the scriptures teach. James 1:13-15 says: "When tempted, no one should say, 'God is tempting me.' For God cannot be tempted by evil, nor does he tempt anyone; but each one is tempted when, by his own evil desire, he is dragged away and enticed [It is Satan who does enticing]. Then, after desire has conceived, it gives birth to sin; and sin, when it is full-grown, gives birth to death."

God does not tempt his children. He does not incite people to sin. God *permits* sin, but he does not *promote* it. The verb (*peirazein*) related to the term traditionally rendered *temptation* in the Lord's Prayer means to *test*. It would be more helpful for us to think of the noun not as temptation, but as *testing*, being on trial. "In the New Testament usage to tempt a person is not so much to seek to seduce him to sin, as it is to test his strength and his loyalty and his ability for service."[177] One might say: "Well, if God is testing us, doesn't that seem like tempting us to do the wrong thing?" To some degree it may. However, the test is not necessarily a bad thing or an evil thing; and even failing the test may not be sinful, generally speaking. The test will reveal our true character and the genuineness of our commitment.

Consider, for example, God's testing of Abraham to offer his son Isaac as a sacrifice (Gen. 22:1-18). The KJV says in Genesis 22:1: "And it came to pass after these things, that God did tempt Abraham...". The

---

[177] Barclay, *The Gospel of Matthew*, Vol. 1, 224.

NIV says: "Some time later God tested Abraham..." This test may be thought of as an experience which could tempt Abraham to be disloyal to God. However, the emphasis is really on the *trial being that which tests* the loyalty and faithfulness of the person; a test which demonstrates the person's true commitment to God and through which God may be glorified and the person, Abraham in this case, may become even more faithful, as refined by fire. A willingness not to sacrifice Isaac would not have been sin in the sense of sparing him. Who would think saving a child would be wrong! So this was not an enticement to do wrong humanly speaking. It was a test of loyalty and faithfulness to God. It was a hard test, to be sure, the kind we would never want to face. *Not to be placed in such a hard testing situation* is what Jesus permits us to pray.[178] And so the *Jerusalem Bible* renders this phrase of the petition: "And do not put us to the test." *Today's English Version* reads: "Do not bring us to hard testing." One ecumenical rendering offers: "Save us from the time of trial."[179] If we were to paraphrase this part of the petition we might say: "O God, please do not place us in testing circumstances," or "O God, please don't be too hard on us," or "please do not allow us to be overcome by testing." All three ideas seem to be a part of the meaning of this petition. James also says: "Blessed is the man who perseveres under trial, because when he has stood the test, he will receive the crown of life that God has promised to those who love him" (1:12).

We should point out, however, that in this petition, we are not praying to be spared suffering; we are praying to be spared being in situations of such great trial and testing through which we might be disloyal to God. It is not a prayer to avoid all trials outright, but rather a prayer not to be entangled and overpowered by them.[180] David Jeremiah has written: "In a sense, this petition is a beautiful confession of our own weakness..."[181] Ivor Powell conveys this truth in his para-

---

[178] Support for this understanding is given in Wesley 341, Vine 1119, and Marvin Vincent 43-44.

[179] International Consultation on English Texts, 1; English Language Liturgical Consultation, 13.

[180] Ayo, 87.

[181] Jeremiah, 161.

phrase of the petition: "Lord, I am so weak, do not burden me with something beyond my strength...let me be the best possible; always dependable, useful, and pleasing in thy sight."[182] The petition reveals how *dependent* upon God we need to be in order for us to weather any trials which God does choose to place in our path. Implied in this petition, therefore, is the need to rely upon the Holy Spirit of God to strengthen us and sustain us in all circumstances. Only in this way will we be able to successfully hallow God's name, increase in his kingdom, and do his will.

We have seen that there are at least two levels of meaning to *Lead us not into temptation*. The first is praying not to be led into trials we will be unable to bear. The second is praying that God will enable us to pass safely through any testing of our faith which he chooses to place us through. A third level of meaning which some have suggested is that the temptation or trial of the petition may also refer to the trial of the end times. Eschatologically speaking, this might mean praying that we be able to escape the great tribulation to come upon the whole world or to pass faithfully through it, depending on one's point of view.[183]

The two phrases of the petition provide similar and related ideas regarding protection, but each has a particular emphasis. *Lead us not into temptation* speaks of trials of any kind through which God tests our loyalty. *Deliver us from evil [or the Evil One]*, which we shall discuss more fully in the next chapter, speaks directly to the subject of protection against falling into sin, and specifically to the temptations and attacks of Satan. *Testing* is a more neutral term whereas evil is decidedly negative. One speaks of God's testing, the other of Satan, the source of all evil, and his attempts to seduce believers. God tests, Satan tempts, as we understand and use the term today. *Lead us not into temptation* is a *prayer for leniency*. "O God, please don't be too hard on us." That is the meaning of the first half of the petition.

---

[182] Ivor Powell. *Matthew's Majestic Gospel* (Grand Rapids: Kregel Publications, 1986), 133.

[183] N. T. Wright, 73.

Reasons for Testing

We may ask, however, why does God allow testing? We shall offer several reasons. The first reason, as we've explained, is to test our loyalty, our devotion. The testing reveals what is in our hearts. Second, testing is also permitted by God to make us stronger Christians,[184] to increase our faith. The apostle Peter wrote:

> ...though now for a little while you may have had to suffer grief in all kinds of trials. These have come so that your faith—of greater worth than gold, which perishes even though refined by fire—may be proven genuine and may result in praise, glory and honor when Jesus Christ is revealed (1 Pet. 1:6-7).

"There once was an ant who felt imposed upon, overburdened, and overworked. He was instructed to carry a piece of straw across an expanse of concrete. The straw was so long and heavy that he staggered beneath its weight and felt he would not survive. Finally, as the stress of his burden began to overwhelm him and he began to wonder if life itself was worth it, the ant was brought to a halt by a large crack in his path. There was no way of getting across that deep divide, and it was evident that to go around it would be his final undoing. He stood there discouraged. Then suddenly a thought struck him. Carefully laying the straw across the crack in the concrete, he walked over it and safely reached the other side. His heavy load had become a helpful bridge. The burden was also a blessing."[185] In testing God enlarges and enriches our faith.

God also tests us to refine our character. The ancient patriarch Job came to this understanding when after much suffering and questioning God's intentions through it, he replied to God: "Surely I spoke of things I did not understand...Therefore I despise myself and repent in dust and ashes" (from Job 42:1-6). Jesus explained to the disciples: "I am the true vine, and my Father is the gardener. He cuts off every

---

[184] Barclay, *The Gospel of Matthew* Vol. 1, 225.

[185] Michael P. Green, ed. *Illustrations for Biblical Preaching* (Grand Rapids: Baker Book House, 1982), 380.

branch in me that bears no fruit, while every branch that does bear fruit he prunes so that it will be even more fruitful" (Jn. 15:1-2). In testing God refines our character.

Testing may be used as a means of accomplishing a great purpose of God. In Jesus' suffering and passion upon the cross, God was providing the atoning sacrifice for the sins of the whole world. Jesus passed the test and through him anyone and everyone may be redeemed and granted eternal life. God may have a special plan to be carried out through us which may involve a hard trial. With Jesus we must say: "Yet not as I will, but as you will" (from Mt. 26:36-44).

The cultivation of perseverance to make us more fit for heaven may be God's will for us in allowing suffering. "...we know that suffering produces perseverance; perseverance, character; and character, hope" (Rom. 5:3-4). "Consider it pure joy, my brothers, whenever you face trials of many kinds, because you know that the testing of your faith develops perseverance. Perseverance must finish its work so that you may be mature and complete, not lacking anything" (Jas. 1:2-4; see also 2 Pet. 1:5-8).

One of the devotionals in *Our Daily Bread* a few years ago told about the "gator aid" given to enlisted men in a Florida training camp during World War II. "The daily training for the GIs included a run through an obstacle course. On the final stretch of the endurance test, they had to grab a rope and swing across a broad shallow pool. Under the blazing southern sun the water looked so inviting to the men that most of them soon developed a habit of making it only halfway across the pond, that is, until an enterprising lieutenant made it the new home for a large alligator. From that day on, the recruits left the ground fifteen feet from the water's edge and fell sprawling in the dust on the other side. In the same way, our behavior as Christians must sometimes be shaped by the 'encouragement' of the danger of unfavorable circumstances. Without God's loving correction and discipline we would never develop spiritual strength and endurance. If the Lord didn't permit threatening conditions to come into our lives, we would soon succumb to feelings of self-sufficiency and over-confidence."[186] God allows suffering for the cultivation of endurance.

---

[186] *Our Daily Bread* (Grand Rapids: RBC Ministries), Vol. 42, No. 4, July 3, 1997.

Another reason we shall mention why God permits testing is that in it God enables us to be helpers to those who suffer. Paul wrote to the Corinthians: "Praise be to the God and Father of our Lord Jesus Christ, the Father of compassion and the God of all comfort, who comforts us in all our troubles, so that we can comfort those in any trouble with the comfort we ourselves have received from God" (2 Cor. 1:3-4). Testing cultivates comforters.

Through trials God tests our loyalty to him. Testing is designed to increase our faith and refine our character. It may be used as a means of accomplishing a great purpose. Tests develop spiritual perseverance, thereby making us more fit for heaven. They help us to be comforters, agents of God's consolation. Of course, in some cases, we may not know the reason why God allows certain things to happen. We must respect and accept his will (Deut. 29:29).

Words of Assurance

We've learned that the meaning of temptation is *testing* and that the first phrase of the petition, *Lead us not into temptation*, is a *prayer for leniency*: "O God, please don't be too hard on us." We've explored reasons why God permits the testing. It may be helpful at this point to offer a few words of assurance from the scriptures which would be good to remember when facing trying circumstances.

Jesus sympathizes with us in our trials. Hebrews 4:15 says: "For we do not have a high priest who is unable to sympathize with our weakness, but we have one who has been tempted in every way, just as we are—yet was without sin." Hebrews 2:18 affirms that Jesus understands. "Because he himself suffered when he was tempted, he is able to help those who are being tempted."

Our Savior intercedes on our behalf. Hebrews 7:25 says: "Therefore he is able to save completely those who come to God through him, because he always lives to intercede for them" (see also Heb. 9:24).

Jesus sends his Spirit to help us. From Romans 8:26-27 we read: "...the Spirit helps us in our weakness. We do not know what we ought to pray for, but the Spirit himself intercedes for us with groans that words cannot express. And he who searches our hearts knows the mind of the Spirit, because the Spirit intercedes for the saints in accordance with God's will." It should be some comfort to realize that the godliest person we know may suffer severe testing, as illustrated by the life of Job.

The trials will not be beyond the believer's strength. 1 Corinthians 10:13 explains: "No temptation [that is, testing] has seized you except what is common to man. And God is faithful; he will not let you be tempted beyond what you can bear. But when you are tempted, he will also provide a way out so that you can stand up under it."

God is in control. He will be lenient. He can protect us from ruin. He knows how to rescue us from trials (2 Pet. 2:9). Charles Wesley penned:

> In every fiery hour
> Display thy guardian power,
> Near in our temptation stay,
> With sufficient grace defend,
> Bring us through the evil day,
> Make us faithful to the end.[187]

O God, thank you for your leniency.
Please don't be too hard on us.

---

[187] Osborn, 179.

Chapter Sixteen

Pleading for Deliverance

Petition Six, Part Two

In 1893 the Norwegian artist Edvard Munch painted a work called "The Scream." An example of expressionistic art, the painting shows a person on a bridge with hands held to the ears and mouth open in what may be a drawn-out howl. The person's gender and age are not discernible. Two other anonymous figures are placed in the background also on the bridge. They may symbolize the indifference of the world to the private anguish of the subject.[188] The lines radiating outward from the tormented person's head seem to accentuate and continue the piercing cry in a pattern of clambering shock waves.[189]

In this work, Munch used visual symbols to express the inner anguish of existence. It is this painting which Ravi Zacharias, a Christian philosopher, used for the dust jacket of his 1996 book, *Deliver Us From Evil (Restoring the Soul in a Disintegrating Culture)*. For Zacharias this art work captures a profound truth about today's world. There is an anxiety which pervades much of Western culture, a despair brought about by a shift in the way people think. That shift has led to all kinds of expression of evil in the world, a world crying out for some sense of meaning, identity and coherence. The Munch painting and Zacharias' thought help us understand why the second part of the last petition of the Lord's Prayer is more than a mild request; it is an *urgent plea*. "Deliver us from evil" is an alarm bell sounding forth the need for divine assistance, protection, and rescue. It is a *pleading for deliverance* from evil.

---

[188] Edmund Burke Feldman. *Varieties of Visual Experience* (Englewood Cliffs, New Jersey: Prentice-Hall, 1967), 187.

[189] William Fleming. *Arts and Ideas*, third ed. (New York: Holy, Rinehart & Winston, Inc., n.d.), 511.

Categories of Evil

Many interpreters agree there are three categories of evil included in this petition. They are: the evil which springs from our sinful nature; the evil which is a product of the world, our culture; and the evil which the Evil One, Satan, the ultimate source of all evil, places in our paths intentionally to tempt us to sin, to be disloyal to God. God may *test* us; but it is Satan who *tempts* us. The three categories are presented by D. Martyn Lloyd-Jones (1899-1981) as the evil in our hearts, the evil in the world, and the evil one.[190] Luther presented them as the flesh, the world, and the devil.[191] Thomas Watson said we pray to be delivered from evil under a threefold notion: from the evil in our heart (Heb. 3:12), from Satan (Mt. 13:19), and from the evil of the world (Gal. 1:4).[192]

The Evil From Within. Watson, in speaking of the evil from within ourselves, within our hearts,[193] cites James 1:14-15: "but each one is tempted when, by his own evil desire, he is dragged away and enticed. Then, after desire has conceived, it gives birth to sin; and sin, when it is full-grown, gives birth to death." The Apostle Paul refers to this inner evil as humanity's *sinful nature*. He wrote to the Roman Christians: "I do not understand what I do. For what I want to do I do not do, but what I hate I do. And if I do what I do not want to do I agree that the law is good. As it is, it is no longer I myself who do it, but it is sin living in me. I know that nothing good lives in me, that is, in my sinful nature. For I have the desire to do what is good, but I cannot carry it out. For what I do is not the good I want to do, no, the evil I do not want to do—this I keep on doing" (Rom. 7:15-19). Paul's position is that all people are sinful; no one is righteous (Rom. 3:10); all sin and fall short of the glory of God (Rom. 3:23). All have a sinful nature which gives rise to evil.

---

[190] Lloyd-Jones Vol. Two, 77.
[191] *Luther's Works* Vol. 21, 147.
[192] Watson, 326.
[193] Ibid., 258.

Evil which arises from within, from the sinful nature, causes injury to the self and to others. Some of the acts which result from the sinful nature Paul catalogued in his letter to the Galatians: "sexual immorality, impurity and debauchery; idolatry and witchcraft; hatred, discord, jealousy, fits of rage, selfish ambition, dissensions, factions and envy; drunkenness, orgies, and the like" (5:19-21). Luther's list of the sins of the flesh include unchastity, laziness, gluttony, drunkenness, greed, deceitfulness, fraud, and deception against a neighbor.[194] It is therefore appropriate that we should pray for God's deliverance from the evil which arises from our own sinful inclinations, that fellowship with God may not be broken, and that we may increase in his kingdom and more successfully accomplish his will.

> With mine enemies surrounded,
> Sin, the world, and Satan's snare,
> Let me never be confounded,
> Tempted more than I can bear:
> Rather from the dread occasion,
> Thy poor helpless creature hide,
> Bind the sinful inclination,
> Turn my stronger foe aside.[195]

O God, deliver us from the evil within.

The Evil of the World. The second category of evil is the evil in/of the world, the diocese of Satan as Watson referred to it.[196] Luther classified many of the evils of the world, including hate, envy, enmity, violence, injustice, revenge, cursing, slander, arrogance, power.[197] In his writing Zacharias' interest here was on the *ideas* upon which peoples' actions are based. If the *ideas* the world espouses are not Godly, it is little wonder the behavior of the world follows suit. "For the wisdom of this world is foolishness in God's sight" (1 Cor. 3:19).

---

[194] Janzow, 94.

[195] Osborn, 185.

[196] Watson, 258; see also I Peter 5:8, John 14:30.

[197] Janzow, 94.

In this post modern era, truth is considered extinct. Values are viewed as transient and relative.[198] The combination of extracting religious views from public discourse (secularization) with the belief that all religious systems are equally valid (pluralization), and with the imprisonment of religious belief (privatization), has resulted in a culture which has no aim, no identity, no coherence, that is, no ideational or ideological glue to hold it together. There are those who would discard all religious belief and even the United States Constitution, and advocate starting from scratch. Martin Luther prayed: "O Lord, bring it to pass that the flesh and the world shall not seduce us."[199] We will add: "Deliver us from the evil of the world."

The Evil One. The third category of evil from which we seek divine protection is deliverance from the Evil One, Satan. *Evil (tou ponerou)* in the Lord's Prayer is a neuter noun but it has a masculine ending. This has given rise to a debate as to the most appropriate translation of the term. Consequently, several versions of the Bible (KJV, CEV, NASB, ESV, and RSV) render the term *evil*, while others (NIV, NCV, NLT, TEV, The Jerusalem Bible, and the NRSV) say *the Evil One*. Evil means destruction, injury, wickedness, sorrow. In the petition it seems fair to say that the term refers to evil in every shape and form and the Evil One. Who is this Evil One, and how may Christians guard against him?

The Evil One is portrayed in the Bible as an active personal power, in opposition to God, not as an abstract principle or force.[200] He is called the prince of this world (Jn. 14:30) for it is here where he operates. He "prowls around like a roaring lion looking for someone to devour" (1 Pet. 5:8). "His chief aim," wrote Luther, "is to make us discard both God's Word and His works, to tear us away from faith, hope, and love, to draw us into unbelief, false security, and stubborn impenitence, or else to drive us into despair, denial of God, blasphemy against

---

[198] Ravi Zacharias. *Deliver Us From Evil: Restoring the Soul in a Disintegrating Culture* (Dallas: Word Publishing, 1996), 215.

[199] *Luther's Works*, Vol. 51, 180.

[200] Barclay, *The Gospel of Matthew*, Vol. 1, 225.

Him, and countless other horrible sins. These are the devil's trap and nets, or more exactly, the most venomously poisoned 'fiery darts' (Eph. 6:16) which not flesh and blood but Satan shoots into our hearts."[201] The two names most commonly used in the Bible for the Evil One are the devil and Satan. Each conveys particular characteristics of our "ancient foe," as Martin Luther described him in the first stanza of "A Mighty Fortress is Our God."

> For still our ancient foe
> Doth seek to work us woe;
> His craft and power are great;
> And, armed with cruel hate,
> On earth is not his equal.

The *Devil* (*diabolos*) means tempter, deceiver, or slanderer. From *diabolos* we acquire the familiar word diabolical. In Matthew 4:1-11 is recorded the scene in which the Devil confronts Jesus in the desert. Knowing Jesus was hungry the Devil tempted him to turn stones into bread. Jesus responded with words from scripture: "Man does not live on bread alone, but on every word that comes from the mouth of God" (Deut. 8:30). Then the Devil tempted him to display his powers, to show off and feed his ego by jumping off the highest point of the Temple. Jesus replied with another citation from scripture: "Do not put the Lord your God to the test" (Deut. 6:16). Finally, exasperated, the Devil tempted Jesus with power and glory if he would worship him. With force Jesus said: "Away from me, Satan! For it is written: Worship the Lord your God, and serve him only" (Deut. 6:13). In what form the Devil appeared to Jesus we do not know. What we do know is the Evil One is the diabolical enemy. He tempts believers to be disloyal to God.

Satan is the other most well-known name for the Evil One. Satan is a Hebrew word (*Satan*) meaning adversary, opponent or accuser. In Job 1:6-12 and 2:1-5 is recorded the scene in which God permits his adver-

---

[201] Janzow, 95.

sary to battle for Job's life and allegiance. In Zechariah 3 Satan assumes a similar role, one in which he acts as a prosecuting attorney and brings an accusation against the high priest Joshua.

In Isaiah Satan is also called morning star, meaning lightbearer: "How you have fallen from heaven, O morning star, son of the dawn! You have been cast down to the earth...You said in your heart...I will make myself like the Most High" (from Isa.14:12-14). In the KJV *morning star* is personalized as *Lucifer*. The idea of Satan as a *lightbearer* is congruent with the description of him in Ezekiel in which he was composed of what looked like brilliantly reflecting gems. It would be difficult for us fully to comprehend the nature of this heavenly attendant. Satan may have been an angel (Jude 9, Rev.12:7-9) with the archangel Michael as his chief foe.

After being cast out of the heavenly realm, the earth and the air were and are Satan's sphere of limited activity (Eph. 2:1-2). He introduces doubt, denial of God's position and power, and sin, as we know from the account of the fall of Adam and Eve (Gen. 3:1-6). The world system, therefore, is based on primitive desires, greedy ambitions, and glamour (1 Jn. 2:15-17). People are duped into believing such attainments will bring satisfaction and success, only to realize time after time, that love of such desires only leads to internal emptiness and despair and a lessening of love for and reliance upon God. Satan is the adversary of all that is truly Godly and meaningful.

The unusual powers and craftiness with which Satan is allowed to operate to test humanity's desire for and loyalty to God is described by the apostle Paul who told the Corinthians that Satan can masquerade as an angel of light and his evil spirit is embodied in false teachers. Having warned them Paul wrote: "For such men are false apostles, deceitful workmen, masquerading as apostles of Christ. And no wonder, for Satan himself masquerades as an angel of light. It is not surprising, then, if his servants masquerade as servants of righteousness. Their end will be what their actions deserve" (2 Cor. 11:13-15; see also Mk. 13:22, 1 Tim. 4:1). Moreover, from the Genesis 3 account we recall that Satan appeared as a serpent. Who knows in how many ways he presents himself to people to try to thwart the plan and purpose of

Pleading for Deliverance

God? Who knows how many ways he tries to deceive well-intended people from being fully committed to God?

The Evil One is also called *Beelzebub*. In Matthew 12 we read of the Pharisees who accused Jesus of healing people by the power of the Evil One. The Pharisees said: "It is only by Beelzebub, the prince of demons, that this fellow drives out demons" (Mt. 12:24). Jesus said he drove out demons by the Spirit of God (Mt. 12:25-29; see also Mark 3:22-27). The Old Testament spelling, *Baalzebub*, is cited in 2 Kings 1:2-6, 16. He was a Philistine god, believed by them to be the creator and controller of flies. Consequently, Baalzebub means "lord of the flies." From Jesus' reply in the Matthew 12 passage, we conclude that he believed in a kingdom of evil spirits or demons under its ruler. Fortunately for us, Jesus came "to destroy the devil's work" (1 Jn. 3:8-9), to counter the temptations, deceptions, and the demonic activity in the world by the Evil One. This is the theme of the third stanza of Luther's chorale text.

> And though this world, with devils filled,
> Should threaten to undo us,
> We will not fear, for God hath willed
> His triumph through us.
> The prince of darkness grim,
> We tremble not for him;
> His rage we can endure,
> For lo! his doom is sure;
> One little word shall fell him.

O God, Deliver us from the Evil One!

Deliverance. The term *deliver* (*rhusai*) literally means *rescue*, or as Barth rendered the petition: "snatch us from the jaws" of the Evil One.[202] The second clause of the petition may be viewed, therefore, as a *pleading for deliverance*. It is a *crying out* to God to save us from the

---

[202] Barth, *Prayer*, 84.

evil which is derived from within the very nature of sinful humanity. It is a plea to be rescued from the clutches of the secularist mindset of the world, with its resultant values and expressions. There is an *urgency* which characterizes this petition. "O God, *please* deliver us from the evil which springs from our sinful nature. *Rescue* us from the evil of the world. *Snatch* us from the jaws of the Evil One."

Countering Evil

Ravi Zacharias urges that in order to restore health to the soul of society there must be a restoration of the soul within individuals.[203] In order to confront the problem of wickedness in the world we must first confront the problem of the evil within the human soul. Each person must come face to face with his or her own sin and choose whether or not to submit to the rebirthing of the spirit which only faith in Jesus Christ can effect.

In order to counter the evil of the world, in order to be able to discern what ideas and behaviors are Godly, Christians must affirm the authority of God's written Word, absorb themselves in this preserved body of truth, and apply its principles in the everyday. The scriptures provide what is missing in the world: a body of truth, moral points of reference. They describe not only the condition of the soul, but also how deliverance from evil may be accomplished in the world. The scriptures were Jesus' instrument to counter evil in the wilderness. Knowledge and appropriate usage of the Bible can help eradicate false ideas that are the root causes of the evil in and of the world.[204]

Christians, more than some believe or may wish to acknowledge, are participants in a war of the spirit (Eph. 6:12). In order for there to be deliverance from the evil within us, Christians should follow the Apostle Paul's admonition to "keep in step with the Spirit" (Gal. 5:25). If the fruit of the spirit is the antithesis of the acts of the sinful nature, then we must intentionally surrender ourselves increasingly to the Holy Spirit's control, allowing God to cultivate within us the spiritual virtues

---

[203] Zacharias, 148.

[204] Ibid., 209.

and graces. Jesus prayed for us: "My prayer is not that you take [my disciples] out of the world but that you protect them from the evil one...My prayer is not for them alone. I pray also for those who will believe in me through their message" (Jn. 17:15, 20).

Certainly, on our own we cannot win the battle. We must claim the power of the living Christ whose death broke the grip of sin in the lives of all who trust in him. The Holy Spirit, whom he imparts to reside in and empower the lives of believers, can and will help to guard against temptation and deception by sensitizing believers' minds and emotions to that which is not of God. Jesus Christ will win the battle through us, if we let him. Stanza two of Luther's hymn captures this truth.

> Did we in our own strength confide,
> Our striving would be losing;
> Were not the right man on our side,
> The man of God's own choosing.
> Dost ask who that may be?
> Christ Jesus, it is He,
> Lord Sabaoth His name,
> From age to age the same,
> And He must win the battle.

On a day-to-day basis God has provided Christians with the means to combat the attacks of the Evil One (2 Tim. 4:16-18). The most eloquent and stirring passage of scripture which describes this defense mechanism is Ephesians 6:11-17.

> Put on the full armor of God so that you can stand against the devil's schemes. For our struggle is not against flesh and blood, but against the powers of this dark world and against the spiritual forces of evil in the heavenly realms. Therefore put on the full armor of God, so that when the day of evil comes, you may be able to stand your guard, and after you have done everything, to stand. Stand firm then, with the belt of truth buckled around your waist, with the breastplate of righteous in place, and with your feet filled with readiness that comes from the

gospel of peace. In addition to all this, take up the shield of faith with which you can extinguish all the flaming arrows of the evil one. Take the helmet of salvation and the sword of the Spirit, which is the word of God.

Above all, Christians are wise to remember the example of Jesus' encounter with the Evil One in the desert as a general guide for engaging successfully in the battle of the spirit. Our Lord was filled with and relied upon the Holy Spirit to sustain and protect; and he quoted and leaned upon the Holy Scriptures. With God's Spirit dwelling within (1 Pet. 1:5) and the preserved Word in our minds and on our lips we may resist the onslaught of the enemy (1 Pet. 5:9). Even though we may walk through valleys of deep darkness we need not fear evil (Ps. 23:4). We may rest in the one who conquered evil. *Christus Victor!* Moreover, at our disposal is all the good we may do to overcome evil (Rom. 12:21), to help a world screaming for meaning. Jesus came to rescue us from evil (Gal. 1:4). We can and we must lean on him for our protection. Greater is he who is in us than the one who is in the world (1 Jn. 4:4).

O God, deliver us from the Evil One!

Chapter Seventeen

Praising God

The Closing Doxology

We come now to the closing statement of the Lord's Prayer: *For thine is the kingdom, and the power, and glory, for ever. Amen* (KJV). The prayer began with a *preface*, addressing God: *Our Father in heaven.* It included *six petitions*, three which focused on divine concerns (God's name, God's kingdom, God's will), and three which dealt with matters of human need (provisions, pardon, and protection). The prayer concludes with an *ascription of praise, a postscript* if you will. What is the meaning of this statement? What is its function in the prayer?

If we were to reword the closing in today's language it might say: "For the kingdom and the power and the glory are yours forever." In light of what we've learned previously about the prayer, a paraphrase and expansion of the closing statement might be the following.

> The *kingdom* and *will* of which we have spoken in our petitions are your kingdom and will, O Lord. They are not ours. *You* are the *sovereign* One. We affirm this. For your rule and purpose within our lives now and eternally, we praise your Holy Name forever.

> The *power* by which you provide for our needs, forgive our sins, and protect us from evil and the Evil One, is your power, O Lord. We affirm this. *You* are the Omnipotent One. We can do *nothing* except by your strength. For the power by which you created and sustain us, for the power by which you raised our Lord Jesus and will raise us on the last day, for the power by which the Evil One will be vanquished, we praise your Holy Name forever.

The *glory*, the *honor*, and the *praise* which is deserved for the coming of your *kingdom*, for the *accomplishment* of your *will*, and for your *provisions, pardon* and *protection*, we give to *you* alone, not to ourselves, not to human achievement, not to chance. All the honor is due only to you, O Lord. We affirm this, and will praise your Holy Name forever.

So we see that the Lord's Prayer ends where it began. Whereas it began with *hallowed be thy name*, it ends with *thine* is the glory. Whereas it began with *thy kingdom come*, it ends with *thine is the kingdom*. It began with *thy will be done*; it ends with *thine is the power*. It began with *on earth as it is in heaven*. It ends with *forever*.[205] The prayer begins and ends with honoring the name of God. In the coming of God's kingdom his eternal *sovereignty* is revealed and exercised. In the doing of his will and providing for our needs, God's eternal power is made manifest. In all of the above God's eternal *majesty* and *splendor* are made known, his eternal *glory* established and attributed.[206] These are the meanings of the closing statement of our Lord's prayer. What *purpose* does it serve?

It provides the prayer with a concluding *doxology*. It is a "paean of praise to God which must break forth from us all when we are overwhelmed by the goodness of God, who is able to do far more abundantly than all we ask or think."[207] This expression of praise is not included in most versions of the Bible. Only in the KJV, the NKJV, and the NASB does it appear. And of course it is found in the worship books of most denominations because of its long-standing and revered use in Christian liturgy. The reason for it not being included in most versions is because it is not found in the oldest manuscripts scholars have to translate. Evidently the earliest appearance of it was in the second century in the early church manual, *The Didache*, in which is found a shorter form: "For thine is the power and the glory forever." It is believed that in the early church this statement was added for use in worship services as a *response*; the idea being that the celebrant would have prayed the prayer

---

[205] Patterned after David Jeremiah, 173.

[206] Ibid.

[207] Thielicke, 147.

on behalf of the people, to which they would respond: "For thine is the kingdom and the power and the glory for ever. Amen." It certainly seems to be a logical addition for use in worship. The prayer would seem incomplete to end with evil. Not only does the closing doxology provide a fitting closure to the prayer, it also provides for a closing *summary* or *abridgement* (kingdom, power, and glory) of the *attributes* and *work* of God included in the petitions. John Wesley commented: "The conclusion of this divine prayer, commonly called the Doxology, is a solemn thanksgiving, a compendious acknowledgment of the attributes and works of God."[208] If indeed this doxology was a congregational *response*, the people then had a part in affirming and giving thanks for the whole of the message of the prayer. *For thine is the kingdom and the power and the glory forever* echoes what was prayed before, as well as serving as a vehicle of praise. Moreover, Matthew Henry said it is a "form of plea to enforce the foregoing petitions."[209] Arthur Pink (1886-1952) adds: "teaching us to back up our request with scriptural reasons or arguments."[210] In addition, the three-fold nature of the doxology (kingdom, power and glory) reminds us of the triune personage of God.

Evidently this doxological phrase was modeled after King David's doxology recorded in 1 Chronicles 29:10-13, offered in *response* to the willingness of the Israelite leaders to support the construction of the temple. David proclaimed the *glory* of God by listing some of God's attributes (emphases added).

> Yours, O Lord, is the *greatness* and the *power* and the *glory* and the *majesty* and the *splendor*, for everything in heaven and earth is yours. Yours, O Lord, is the *kingdom*; you are exalted as *head* over all. Wealth and honor come from you; you are the ruler of all things. In your hands are *strength* and *power* to exalt and give strength to all. Now our God, we give you *thanks*, and *praise* your glorious name.

---

[208] Wesley, 341.

[209] *Matthew Henry's Commentary On the Whole Bible* Vol. 5, 61.

[210] Arthur W. Pink. *An Exposition of the Sermon on the Mount* (Grand Rapids: Baker Book House, 1982), 165.

UNITED IN PRAYER

The tradition of providing for congregational responses is long standing. It continues today even in the use of our doxologies. In some traditions the *Gloria Patri* is sung in response to Words of Assurance, for they are truly good news. The *Doxology* is sung as an expression of thanksgiving and praise in response to God's many gifts bestowed upon us. Not only so, because the words *for ever* are attached, the expression of praise anticipates the doxologies which will be offered God throughout all ages to come. The closing doxology of the Lord's Prayer takes us beyond the earthly scene of the prayer proper. It anticipates the perfect rest prepared for us—the eschatological and eternal. It looks forward to dimensions of God's kingdom, power, and glory. John Wesley captured this aspect of the postscript in stanza nine of his *A Paraphrase on the Lord's Prayer*.

> Blessing and honour, praise and love,
> Co-equal, co-eternal Three,
> In earth below, in heaven above,
> By all thy works be paid to thee.
> Thrice Holy! Thine the kingdom is,
> The power omnipotent is thine;
> And when created nature dies,
> Thy never-ceasing glories shine.[211]

We may also consider the closing praise is included for our benefit. Many may pray the Lord's Prayer, but with troubled hearts. Praise lifts us above our trials, focuses our attention on God who desires to deliver us. It extends our vision to the ultimate joy and reward for our faithfulness and service. It helps us to be more Godly-minded and to guard against self-centeredness, either as pity or glory as the case may be. Helmut Thielicke expressed this well.

> To praise God means to see things from the perspective of their end, to view them in the light of the great goals and fulfillments of God. That's why Paul could sing at midnight, despite

---
[211] Wesley, 343.

his torn and heavy spirit. That's why he could not help but sing, for he knew that if in all his physical and mental pain, he simply dared to praise God —despite the obvious circumstances, despite his reason and his nerves— this end of the warp of God would rise up within his soul and the kingdom of God would surround him in the midst of the damp, dark dungeon.[212]

The doxology enables us to end the prayer, and all prayer to be modeled after it, with praise.

To review, the inclusion of *For thine is the kingdom and the power and the glory forever* enables us to praise God for all he is and does. It enables us to affirm, to repeat in a way, the petitions which have been or may otherwise be offered in our personal prayers. It may be considered, therefore, as a plea that our prayers be heard. As such it may be a suitable closing for any of our individually offered prayers.

The doxology is a kind of *thanksgiving* for all of God's will and work. It serves as a *summary* or an *abridgement* of the attributes of God. This postscript is also a form of *reinforcement*. It teaches us that "our prayers are founded on God alone, that we may not rely on our own merits"[213] for the advancement of God's work or the provision of our needs. Finally, the closing praise is a salve for the soul. It lifts us up from ourselves into the hands and promises of God. It provides *hope* and *assurance*.

One final word we need to make about the prayer concerns the concluding *Amen* as it is given in the KJV and used regularly by parishioners in worship. The use of Amen in worship has a long tradition as well. We read in the Old Testament, for example, that it was the peoples' *response* to the psalm of thanksgiving offered by Asaph and his associates when King David had the Ark of the Covenant brought to Jerusalem and placed in the tent of meeting (1 Chr. 16:36). In Nehemiah 8:5-6 we read of the great revival under Ezra. When he stood on a platform, opened the Book the Law and praised the Lord,

---

[212] Thielicke, 155.

[213] *Calvin's Commentaries* Vol. XVI, 329.

the people responded: "Amen! Amen!"

In the New Testament (1 Cor. 14:16, 2 Cor. 1:19-20) we hear of the early church's usage of the Amen as an expression of *agreement* to what someone else had said, or as a response of *affirmation* and *commitment* to another's remarks. In some churches today it is common to hear parishioners express an Amen audibly during the sermon when a matter of importance to them has been mentioned. Sometimes people will say Amen after a meaningful musical offering. The selective use of Amens after singing hymns is appropriate when the hymn sung is one of strong affirmation or when its text is a prayer. *Amen* means *so be it, let it be so,* or *let it be granted.* In terms of its use after the Lord's Prayer, it means, *may everything I prayed come to pass. Let it be so. O God, grant these petitions.* The Amen is a kind of *punctuation mark*, an *emphatic* conclusion, one which knits together all of the previous requests and expressions and *sums* up the *sincerity* of the petitioner. The Amen is an expression of unquestioning faith. It expresses both *fervent desire* that all petitions be granted, and it indicates the belief that God will hear and answer according to his will. It shall be so.[214] Thus the Amen is a response of affirmation, punctuation mark, and a summation device. It is a kind of seal of agreement, ratification and acceptance of God's sovereignty and care.

In the closing doxology we learn that all our prayers should end in praise, for it is God who will execute his will and who provides for his people. How thankful we should be for him who cared enough to send the very best into our lives, Jesus his Son, in whom we trust as the bridge between ourselves and God the Father. To him be the glory forever and ever.

---

[214] Pink, 165.

Chapter Eighteen
Summarizing the Prayer
With Helps for Teaching the Prayer to Children

Our Father in the heavens:

May your name be hallowed;
May your kingdom come;
May your will be done on earth
as it is in heaven.

Give us this day our daily bread.
Forgive us our sins
as we forgive those who sin against us.
Spare us severe testing
and rescue us from the evil one.

For the kingdom, the power, and the glory
are yours forever. Amen.

Copyright Setting Peter E. Roussakis 2007

Now that we have quite thoroughly provided an understanding and interpretation of Jesus' prayer, it may be useful to try to summarize this great body of truth, that which may be useful for introducing parishioners and others to the prayer's significance, after which we shall close by relating some of the values of understanding and praying the prayer. Included here will be a paraphrase of each part of the prayer suitable for teaching the meanings of the prayer with anyone, and especially for teaching children a guide is provided.

Overview

The context of the Lord's Prayer is Jesus' Sermon on the Mount, a collection of our Lord's *primary sayings* within which he exposed the wrong motives of the Pharisees in their practices of almsgiving, fasting and prayer. Jesus offered his instruction on the correct way to pray. Appropriate prayer should begin by *addressing God*, followed by praying for the fulfillment of God's work in the world: hallowing God's name, advancing his kingdom, and doing his will. These *petitions* may then be followed by making requests for human needs: daily provisions, pardon for sins, and protection against all forms of evil. A closing *ascription of praise* to God provides a suitable ending.

The Preface

The preface, *Our Father in heaven*, serves as an invocation, the address of the prayer. In the preface we learn something of the *title* and the *attributes* of God, something about the associations between divinity and humanity. The title *Father* indicates God is *personal, approachable, available, caring*. The term *in heaven* suggests God is sovereign and conveys his *otherness*, his separateness. *Father* stresses the nearness of God. *In heaven* communicates the transcendence of God. The term *Father* indicates an intimate personal relationship is possible between God and us. God is our Father by his act of creation (Mal. 2:10), election (Eph. 1:4) and adoption (Eph. 1:5-7). Martin Luther wrote the following poetic interpretation.[215]

> Our Father, Thou in heav'n above,
> Who biddest us to dwell in love,
> As brethren of one family,
> And cry for all we need to Thee;
> Teach us to mean the words we say,
> And from the inmost heart to pray.

---

[215] This and all other stanzas listed in this summary are taken from Luther's poetic interpretation ("Vater unser im Himmelreich") of the Lord's Prayer as translated by Catherine Winkworth. See note 142.

Petition One

In today's language the first petition, *Hallowed be thy name*, combined with the preface, might read: *Our Father in heaven, may your name be hallowed.* The term *hallow* means to treat a person or thing as *holy*, different, separate, special, *set apart* from everyday usage. John Calvin rendered this petition: "May thy name be sanctified."[216] In Israelite tradition someone's name was synonymous with one's character. Therefore, to *misuse* God's name is an act of dishonoring God, an act of marring the reputation of God. Christians are admonished to use God's name with reverence.

> All hallow'd be Thy name, O Lord!
> Oh let us firmly keep Thy Word,
> And lead, according to Thy name,
> A holy life, untouch'd by blame;
> Let no false teaching do us hurt—
> All poor deluded souls convert.

Petition Two

In contemporary usage the second petition, *Thy kingdom come*, may read: *May your kingdom come.* One of the ways God is portrayed in scripture is as a king, a great and glorious sovereign (e.g. Psalm 47:7-8). His kingdom is two-dimensional, earthly and heavenly, both present and future, already and not yet. The *present*, earthly, already dimension is called by Thomas Watson the *kingdom of God's grace*.[217] Watson terms the future, heavenly, not yet category as the *kingdom of God's glory*.[218] We must enter the kingdom of God's grace in order to be able to pass to the kingdom of God's glory. The term *come* literally suggests come into being instantaneously. "Let it happen, let it take place." Therefore, the kingdom of God's grace *comes* when the spirit of Jesus Christ enters and takes up residence in a person's inner being. The Spirit comes when persons acknowl-

---

[216] John Calvin, *Calvin's Commentaries* Volume XVI, 318.
[217] Watson, 59.
[218] Ibid.

edge Jesus Christ as their personal Savior and Lord (John 14:16-17, Acts 2:38). Following entering the kingdom of God's grace, believers are obligated to *increase*, to *progress*, to *advance*, to *grow* spiritually, that they may be useful for God's service and persevere in the faith until they are gathered into the kingdom of God's glory in the hereafter.

> Thy kingdom come! Thine let it be
> In time, and through eternity!
> O let Thy Holy Spirit dwell
> With us, to rule and guide us well;
> From Satan's mighty power and rage
> Preserve Thy Church from age to age.

Petition Three

Thy will be done on earth as it is in heaven may be rendered *May your will be done on earth as it is in heaven*. To be in the kingdom is to do the will of God. The scope of this petition includes God's *predestined will*, carrying out the *plan* of God for the world, that the kingdom may come into peoples' lives and that they may increase and persevere in faith. It includes God's *prescribed will*, obedience to his precepts, living holy lives. It also includes God's *personal will* for each believer, what God's will and work is for each person in the kingdom. The *manner* of doing God's will is suggested by the phrase *on earth as it is in heaven*. Thomas Watson suggested that means *in the same way as* God's will is done by the angels in heaven: regularly, entirely, sincerely, willingly, fervently, skillfully, obediently, and constantly.[219]

> Thy will be done on earth, O Lord,
> As where in heaven Thou art adored!
> Patience in time of grief bestow,
> Obedience true through weal and woe;
> Strength, tempting wishes to control
> That thwart Thy will within the soul.

---

[219] Ibid., 157-162.

The Second Group of Petitions

The second group of three petitions focuses on *human needs*. Since we have aligned ourselves with God's program, desiring to hallow his name, to enter and increase in his kingdom, and do his will, we may pray for our *daily, temporal needs, forgiveness of sins, protection from severe trial and from the Evil One*. These petitions, therefore, demonstrate our complete *dependence* upon God for all things. *God* is the primary cause of all our benefits. God desires to meet our needs because he loves us, because he is interested in the totality of our lives, and so that his glory may be revealed in us. He desires that we be effective disciples and so he willingly provides for our physical, spiritual and social well-being. There is an *intentional connection* between God's *program* and the *provisions* needed for effective discipleship. Moreover, the manner in which we make our requests, in the *imperative (give, forgive, lead not, deliver)*, suggests there is an *urgency* attached to them. The urgency is related to the importance of accomplishing God's work, because there are so many who have yet to come to faith and commitment. Those who do not will be held accountable for their unbelief (Heb. 3:19, 4:12-13). Souls are at stake.

The Plurals

We should also emphasize that implied in each of these requests is the responsibility we share as *receivers* of God's benefits to be concerned about the well-being of others, especially those of the household of faith. We have permission to pray for personal concerns *so long as* we are willing to help others acquire their daily bread, so long as we are willing to forgive the sins of those who may have sinned against us, so long as we guard against living in any ways which could influence others to compromise God's intentions for human moral integrity and purity. We may pray for human needs so long as we accept the obligation to protect others from the entanglements of the world. A genuine regard for others is what our Lord requires of us. We derive this understanding from the *plurals* of the prayer: *Our* Father...Give *us* this day *our* daily bread. Forgive *us our* sins as *we* forgive *those* who sin against *us*. Lead *us* not into temptation, but deliver *us* from evil. These *plurals* emphasize the *communal* nature of the prayer, of the Christian family. It stresses the *relational* character of human life in general. We are *dependent* upon God and *interdependent* of one another. Since we depend on God and one another, we have an obligation to live as God intends and to appreciate and care for our fellow human beings. In our personal lives and in our relations with others we are called to mirror the character of God.

Petition Four

The term *bread* in the fourth petition, *Give us this day our daily bread*, is a figure of speech, *synecdoche*, meaning one thing stands for a whole class of things. Bread stands for all of the *temporal needs* we humans require for living and flourishing. Bread refers to our basic necessities, those things in the everyday which will sustain us and equip us to do God's will. Moreover, although we are not to worship *things*, we should have a healthy appreciation for them as having potential for the accomplishment of the will and work of God. The term *our* provides a *qualification* to our request, however. Because we live in *community* we are obliged to help those who lack temporal benefits. The terms *this day* and *daily* suggest further that there is a *limitation* placed upon us. We should only pray for and appreciate the *minimum* which we need. The limitation is for our benefit and is designed to help guard against *avarice*. Daily, regular dependence upon God is a primary concern of this petition.

> Give us today our daily bread,
> Let us be duly clothed and fed,
> And keep Thou from our homes afar
> Famine and pestilence and war,
> That we may live in godly peace,
> Unvex'd by cares and avarice.

Petition Five

Since the prayer is directed to disciples, the focus of this petition, *Forgive us our debts as we forgive our debtors*, is on seeking forgiveness of sins *after* persons have entered the kingdom of God. Nevertheless, it is not outside the sphere of the subject to discuss God's pardon *when* entering the kingdom of God's grace. That this is apparent is due to the usage by our Lord of the term translated *debts*. *Debts*, a financial term, is an analogue for sins because all persons are in *spiritual debt* to God because of their sins. "All have sinned and fall short of the glory of God" (Romans 3:23) and deserve spiritual and eternal death. The term signifies that all people will be held accountable to God for their lives. Unless the debt is paid, all will be considered in arrears and will be punished.

Fortunately, knowing there was no way we could pay the debt, for payment would mean giving our lives, God in his mercy paid the debt for us in the death and resurrection of the sinless Christ (Heb. 4:15). He made substitutionary atonement for our sins. That is the reason why all humanity owes its life to Jesus, and why all are called to acknowledge and pledge allegiance to him as the Savior of their souls and the Lord of their lives. That is what God asks in return and in response to his gracious offer of redemption (Rom. 10:9) as the requirement for *entering* the kingdom of his grace. God's *condition* for the pardon of our sins *after* we've entered the kingdom is that we forgive the sins of those who have sinned against us. If we claim to be Christian and do not forgive, God will not forgive us. That is the message of the second half of the petition "as we forgive our debtors" and of the warning Jesus added in Matthew 6:14-15 following the prayer proper. It is also the message of the parable of the unmerciful servant recorded in Matthew 18. The importance attached to this condition is that Christians are called to faithfully mirror the character of God in their lives. *Forgiving others* is a witness to non-believers that God truly forgives the penitent. Such behavior advances God's reputation in the world, and promotes the ministry of the Gospel.

> Forgive our sins, that they no more
> May grieve and haunt us as before,
> As we forgive their trespasses
> Who unto us have done amiss;
> Thus let us dwell in charity,
> And serve each other willingly.

Petition Six

The last petition, *Lead us not into temptation, but deliver us from evil [the Evil One]*, has two parts. *Lead us not into temptation* is parallel with *deliver us from evil [the Evil One]* in that both are requests for protection. Each phrase, however, has a specific focus of attention. In the first clause temptation does not refer to solicitation to evil. God may permit us to stumble, but he does not promote wrongdoing or failure. By *temptation* is meant *testing, severe trial*. God permits trials to test our loyalty and devotion, as in the examples of Abraham (Gen. 22:1-8) and Job. True character and allegiance are exposed in testing. In this petition, therefore, we are not praying to be spared suffering. Rather, we are praying to be spared being placed in situations of such trial in which we fear we might dishonor God. It is, therefore, a *prayer for leniency. Oh God, please do not be too hard on us!*

Within the second clause of the petition, *deliver us from evil [the Evil One]*, are included *three categories of evil*. The *first* is evil which springs up from our *sinful nature*, as Paul described it (Rom. 7:15-19), and is known by the many sins of the flesh (e.g. Gal. 5:19-21). The second category of evil is the *evil of the world*, its ideas and accepted behaviors. *Secularism* is the reigning world view of humanity, which leaves no room in public discourse or policy making for reference to religion. Post-modern society exists, therefore, without any point of reference, without aim, without direction, without any unifying principle, without hope.

The term *evil* in the Lord's Prayer may also be translated the *Evil One*. In the Bible the Evil One is portrayed as an active personal power, called the prince of this world (Jn.14:30). The *devil*, meaning tempter or deceiver, and *Satan*, meaning adversary or accuser, are the two most frequently used biblical terms for this diabolical opponent of Christians. Because of the strength of this ancient foe, and the seriousness of the threat to the well-being and successful witness of Christians, this part of the petition is really a *plea for rescue* from the clutches of this spiritual enemy. In order to be fortified to do battle with the Evil One, Christians are admonished to pray regularly to be delivered, to put on the armor of God (Eph. 6:11-17), and make progress in piety.

Into temptation lead us not,
And when the foe doth war and plot
Against our souls on every hand,
Then, arm'd with faith, oh may we stand
Against him as a valiant host,
Through comfort of the Holy Ghost.

Deliver us from evil, Lord,
The days are dark and foes abroad;
Redeem us from the second death,
And when we yield our dying breath,
Console us, grant us calm release,
And take our souls to Thee in peace.

The Praise

The closing statement of the Lord's Prayer, *For thine is the kingdom and the power and the glory forever*, is an ascription of praise, a *doxology*. In more contemporary parlance it may be rendered: *For the kingdom and the power and the glory are yours forever.* God's sovereignty, power and majesty are extolled. Although the statement is not found in the oldest manuscripts scholars have to translate, the early church may have included it as a fitting congregational response to the prayer proper for use in worship. It was evidently patterned after David's doxology recorded in 1 Chronicles 29:10-13. It also serves as a vehicle of thanksgiving and summation for all which has been said previously. The concluding *Amen* functions as a punctuation mark, a word of affirmation, agreement, and assurance. *Let it be so. Let it be granted. It shall be so.*

Amen! that is, so let it be!
Strengthen our faith and trust in Thee,
That we may doubt not, but believe
That what we ask we shall receive;
Thus in Thy name and at Thy word
We say Amen, now hear us, Lord!

UNITED IN PRAYER

The above concepts may be presented to children, explaining that the prayer has three parts: a *beginning*, followed by *six requests* (the petitions), and an *ending* of praise. By way of introduction to the requests, it is suggested that the teacher discuss the first group of petitions one at a time, mentioning that each of the first three requests are concerned primarily with God matters: God's name, God's kingdom, and God's will. Then the second group of petitions may be reviewed, explaining they focus primarily on human concerns: our daily needs, forgiveness of sins, and protection from evil. This then would be followed by saying and explaining each phrase of the prayer. A synopsis of how each phrase may be described to the children is given below. While the Lord's Prayer is given in the plural (e.g. *Our* Father...), younger children will grasp the essential meanings of the phrases if for the time being they are explained in the first person. As they grow up the sense of community will be more understandable to them. What follows then are the phrases and their meanings for younger children.

Summarizing the Prayer

Our Father who art in heaven
(Father in heaven,)

Hallowed be thy name
(Help me to use your name respectfully.)

Thy kingdom come
(Come and live in my heart and guide me how to live.)

Thy will be done on earth as it is in heaven
(Help me to know how you want me to live,
and please help me to do it.)

Give us this day our daily bread
(Please help me today with whatever I need.)

Forgive us our debts as we forgive our debtors
(Please forgive me of my sins, and help me to forgive others.)

Lead us not into temptation but deliver us from evil
(Please don't be too hard on me, and protect me from evil.)

*For thine is the kingdom and the power
and the glory forever. Amen.*
(I thank you God for all that you are
and all that you do. Amen.)

Chapter Nineteen
Praying the Lord's Prayer

It has been said that the Lord's Prayer is misnamed, that our Lord would not have prayed this prayer because there was no need for him to pray for forgiveness of sins, and that the prayer may be better labeled the Disciples' Prayer.[220] To be sure, Jesus' need would not have been to confess sins, and the prayer was given for disciples to pray. However, the prayer is truly our Lord's instruction. It is the prayer he formulated for those who would follow him. It is, therefore, the prayer which bears his stamp of ownership and authority, and is very appropriately attributed to him as the source of its formulation. That is the reason for it being called the Lord's Prayer.

Collective Use

Another reason for calling it the Lord's Prayer is derived from the Lukan account of the prayer. Luke 11:1 says: "One day Jesus was praying in a certain place. When he finished, one of his disciples [we would love to know which one] said to him, 'Lord, teach us to pray, just as John taught his disciples.'" As we've mentioned previously, this is significant because it tells us that it was the custom for rabbis to teach their disciples a prayer which would be uniquely theirs, a kind of mark of identity with that rabbi, and which they might use regularly[221]. Moreover, this understanding helps us realize the prayer was intended for group use. The plurals of the prayer tell us directly that the intention of Jesus was for his disciples to pray it together. If Jesus formulated this prayer as one for disciples to pray, then we are instructed and invited by him to pray it as a mark of our identity with and allegiance to him. What a privilege and an honor is ours to know Jesus himself has given us a prayer to pray. We are united together with the original dis-

---

[220] For example, Haddon Robinson. *Jesus' Blueprint for Prayer* (Grand Rapids: RBC Ministries, 1989), 3-4.
[221] William Barclay. *The Gospel of Luke*, 143.

ciples, with those of all ages since, and presently with all believers from every nation and station in life as we pray together these treasured words.

To be sure, the Lord's Prayer is also a guide for praying, or as Michael Youssef termed it, "God's curriculum for Prayer."[222] We will discuss that further below. However, the expressed instruction of Jesus was that we actually *say* the prayer together. The Dutch Reformed theologian Herman Witsius (1636-1708) expounded intensely about this matter in his major treatise on the prayer.

> Undoubtedly, the disciple who made the request did not so much desire to be informed about the manner of praying, as to be furnished with a copy and form of prayer, similar to those which had been given by the Pharisees to their followers, and by John to his hearers. This desire our Lord Jesus cheerfully gratifies, not saying, 'pray nearly in this manner,' but *when ye pray, say*. He does not say, ask that the name of God may be hallowed, that his kingdom may come, and so on,—as he would have done if he had meant it merely as a copy. But he says *when ye pray say, Our Father which art in heaven, hallowed be thy name*, suggesting not the subjects only, or the dispositions, but the words in which our Heavenly Father chooses to be addressed.[223]

To emphasize, Luke 11:2 says: "He said to them, 'When you pray, say......'" Our Lord expects us to *say* this prayer as his disciples and to pray it together. John Stott (1921-2011) concurs: "...he tells us to pray in the plural 'Our Father', and one can scarcely pray that prayer in secret alone."[224] It is clear that Jesus intended the prayer to be prayed by disciples in the group setting and using the words he taught.

---

[222] Michael Youssef. *The Prayer That God Answers: Experiencing the Power and Fullness of The Lord's Prayer* (Nashville: Thomas Nelson Publishers, 2000), 9.

[223] Herman Witsius. *Sacred Dissertations on The Lord's Prayer* (Escondido, CA: The den Dulk Christian Foundation, 1994), 126.

[224] John Stott. *The Message of the Sermon on the Mount* (Downers Grove, IL: Inter-Varsity Press, 1978), 134.

Witsius also explained that rabbis taught their people prayers which would encapsulate a body of truth, perhaps a brief compendium of previously presented and more extensive prayers. Such prayers would be used to summarize and conclude longer prayers given by the rabbi.[225] The *summary prayer* would be prayed by the people, using the exact words the rabbi taught. In today's worship, following an Invocation or Prayer of Intercession offered by the pastor, or as an affirmation of faith, it is appropriate for the congregation to pray the Lord's Prayer.

In ancient church usage, as Witsius points out, it was also customary to pray the Lord's Prayer, after which other prayers might be added.[226] So while its usage is variable, it is clear from the days of Jesus onward, the Lord's Prayer was intended to be prayed by disciples together. Witsius asked: "What prayer can have greater power with the Father than that which came from the lips of the Son, who is the Truth?"[227] We should be ever thankful that Jesus formulated for us a prayer which is *uniquely ours* and for all Christians, past, present and future.

Values and Potentialities

We may say, therefore, that one of the values and potentialities of praying the Lord's Prayer in worship is its *unifying* capacity. Believers in Christ are bonded together in the praying of the prayer our Lord has taught us. Along with Holy Communion and baptism, the Lord's Prayer is truly a symbol of Christian identity and oneness. Praying the prayer together sounds forth the truths contained within it, and awakens Christians' consciousness to the presence of God, to one another, and to their common bond under our Father in heaven. It is "the keynote of all Christian prayers. It is the concert-pitch of the universal heavenly choir of the whole family on earth and in heaven."[228] "Christ gave us the Lord's Prayer to unite us to him and to each other."[229]

---

[225] Witsius, 124-125.

[226] Ibid., 129.

[227] Ibid.

[228] Philip Schaff, *A Christian Cetechism for Sunday Schools and Families*, 29.

[229] Lorraine Kisley. *The Prayer of Fire: Experiencing the Lord's Prayer* (Brewster, Mass: Paraclete Press, 2004), 12.

Other values of praying the Lord's Prayer together in worship or other group settings include it being a means of *confessing and proclaiming our faith.* For as we've demonstrated through the exposition of each phrase of the prayer, our Lord's prayer is the *embodiment* of essential Christian beliefs expressed in a petitionary form, mentioned previously in chapter eleven regarding the biblical *tephillah.*

This combination of petition as profession was the subject of J. Harold Ellens' fine article, *"Communication Theory and Petitionary Prayer."* He made the case that by its very nature and composition the Lord's Prayer is a confession of faith. He described the first section of the prayer in Matthew's account as an affirmation by us in prayer of that which God is and does. The second section (verses 11-13a.) he describes as an affirmation of our human nature as children of God, of the identification of our need for God's redemptive care (e.g. bread [provisions]). It is also a certification of our human need for forgiveness.[230] Section three (verse 13b.) he described as "a doxological summary of all that is affirmed or confessed or celebrated in sections one and two."[231] Ellens suggests, therefore, that the Lord's Prayer is essentially a *declarative prayer, a declaratory profession of faith in petitionary formula.*[232]

To help us appreciate further the *confessional potentiality* of the prayer, we might imagine it recast and amplified as statements of faith. Based on the interpretations given previously, we may offer the following:

> We believe God is our heavenly Father, who planned for our redemption and adopted us into his family. He is above us, yet ever near, powerful and personal, great and gracious, majestic and merciful, holy and helpful.

> We believe God's name is synonymous with his identity and character, and that we should hold his name in highest regard, never misusing it, for to do so is an act of disrespect.

---

[230] Ellens, 52.

[231] Ibid.

[232] Ibid., 52 & 53.

We believe we enter the kingdom of God's grace by faith as we receive Jesus Christ as our Savior and Lord. We understand that we must surrender daily to the Holy Spirit's leading in order to increase and persevere in the kingdom, and so that we may receive a rich welcome in the kingdom of God's glory.

We believe we are privileged to participate in the doing of God's predestined will for this world, that we have an obligation to be faithful in complying with his prescribed will for all people, and that we should seek to know and do God's will for us as individuals and as communities of faith.

We believe we may approach God for our daily needs because he is concerned for our well-being. He desires that we be provided for so that we may enjoy life to the full, and so we may successfully advance his kingdom and do his will. We acknowledge, however, that we should request only what we need, that we should consider the needs of others, and that we should never forget to thank God for all his benefits.

We believe we are in debt to God because we are sinners, that God offered the death and resurrection of Jesus as payment for our debt, and that we must acknowledge Christ as our personal Savior and Lord in order to be justified to enter God's kingdom. After entering we know we must forgive the sins of others as the condition for God's forgiving our on-going sins.

We believe we need to pray for God's protection on a daily basis because of the many challenges and threats to our Christian living. We know God may test us, and so we ask for leniency. We need to put on the full armor of God in order to guard against giving in to our sinful nature, and in order to do battle successfully against the evils of the world and the attacks of the Evil One.

We believe God will have the ultimate victory, that Jesus Christ will return to gather the elect and defeat the Evil One. We believe that the unseen eternal realm belongs to God, that he is the All-Powerful One, and that he deserves all the glory and praise forever and ever. And it shall be so!

To reiterate, the Lord's Prayer is a compendium of the Gospel. When we gather together and pray the prayer we do more than offer a collective prayer to God. Without realizing it, we are *confessing our faith*.[233] In the preface we announce and affirm our relationship with God, our Father. In the petitions we confess our willingness and desire to hallow God's name, to enter and increase and persevere in God's kingdom, and to do his will. We declare our dependency upon God for all things: provision for temporal necessities, pardon for sin, and protection from all manner of evil and the evil one. In the prayer is a summary of many of the elements of the *kerygma*[234] of the early church. In the closing statement of praise we sound forth that God is the greatest!

The text of the Lord's Prayer is a *container of belief*. Praying it is a means of communicating and confessing the belief contained within it. As reciting creeds and singing hymns are circulating media, so in praying the Lord's Prayer is the faith contained within it circulated, transmitted, shared, and a bond cultivated between all who share in the praying. Praying the prayer is a means of *unification* and *proclamation*. The Lord's Prayer has *confessional* value.

There is also *educational* value to the study and praying of the prayer. The great wealth of Christian truth which is compressed into the prayer's phrases has been acknowledged through the centuries by the church. The prayer is an essential source of learning about our faith. Many catechisms have been written for church membership instruction which include the study of the Ten Commandments, the Apostles' Creed, and the Lord's Prayer. We've cited previously

---

[233] A more thorough treatment of this subject is given in Peter E. Roussakis, *Confessing the Compendium: Praying the Lord's Prayer as Confessing Faith* (Burlington, IN: Meetinghouse Press, 2005).

[234] By *kerygma* is meant the body of essential truths of the Gospel message proclaimed by the Gospel writers and in the preaching of the early church, as in the sermons of Peter, Stephen and Paul.

Tertullian's label, *compendium of the whole gospel,* Martin Luther's description of the trilogy of the Catechism, a *digest of doctrine,* and Philip Schaff's characterization of the Lord's Prayer as *the gospel in a nutshell.* From our study of the prayer's meanings, it is clear why these descriptions of the prayer recognize it as a container and summary of a significant body of Christian belief. To examine the prayer's inclusions is to become exposed to this *digest of doctrine.* To pray the prayer is to enable those beliefs to become instilled in believers' minds and hearts. Praying the prayer, therefore, serves as a *mnemonic aid* for learning its contents.

G. Campbell Morgan's comments on the prayer being an example of an *index prayer* help us appreciate its instructional significance.

> The Jewish Rabbis taught the people what were known as index prayers. These consisted of a collection of brief sentences, each one of which suggested a subject of prayer. One of their habits of praying was to take such an index prayer, recite one petition at a time, and elaborate it in the presence of God by carrying out its thought, and endeavoring to express its full intent. In that sense the Lord's Prayer also is an index prayer.[235]

That the Lord's Prayer may be viewed as an example of an index prayer tells us that the contents are an index of themes which when prayed provide an outline of the essential themes of Christian belief and devotion. Teaching and praying the prayer, therefore, assists in passing on the faith to the next generation of believers. The content, outline and use of the Lord's Prayer demonstrate its *confessional, educational* and *transmissional* values.

Another educational value of the Lord's Prayer is the one most often voiced, that it is a model for praying, a *model* which the pattern and outline of the prayer provides. To be sure, the Lord's Prayer is intended to be prayed with other disciples as the Lukan text affirms. However, the words of Jesus prior to the Matthean version, "This, then is how you should pray:...," suggests to us the prayer is also a model for pray-

---

[235] Morgan, 59.

ing. The Lord's Prayer is at one and the same time a prayer to pray and a model prayer. John Stott has commented: "According to Matthew he gave it as a pattern to copy (*Pray then like this*), according to Luke as a form to use (11:2, 'When you pray, say...'). We are not obliged to choose, however, for we can both use the prayer as it stands and also model our own praying upon it."[236] Dietrich Bonhoeffer (1906-1945) punctuated this truth: "Jesus told his disciples not only *how* to pray, but also *what* to say. The Lord's Prayer is not merely the pattern prayer, it is the way Christians *must* pray."[237]

At some point in the latter 1990's during my immersion in the study of the Lord's Prayer, I decided to discipline myself to pattern my private praying after Jesus' instruction. Daily I begin my private prayers with the following extended prayer which blends acknowledgement of the persons and work of the Father, Son and Holy Spirit, with petitions drawn from those of the Lord's Prayer.

> Heavenly Father, thank you for your love and your mercy, your providential care and your plan of salvation, for redeeming us by faith in Christ, and for caring about us all the time. Thank you for your provisions, and I pray for the continuance of them. Thank you for enabling me to be a part of your kingdom and in your service. I pray for your continued help to hallow your name, to increase in your kingdom, to persevere in the faith, and to help others do the same.
>
> Thank you Lord Jesus for being our Savior, our Teacher, Example, and our Friend, for dying on the cross for our sins, for rising from the dead, having victory over Satan and death, and for giving us hope, the promise of our own resurrection. Thank you for your mercy, for opening the way to a right relationship with the Father. I pray for forgiveness of my sins, for a cleansing of my life by the power of your precious blood; and I pray for a filling of your Spirit and love to forgive others.

---

[236] Stott, 145.

[237] Dietrich Bonhoeffer. *The Cost of Discipleship* (New York: The Macmillan Company, 1970), 184.

Thank you Holy Spirit for living within us by faith in Christ, for your power and presence, your comfort and direction. Please strengthen my immediate family [named specifically], our church families, our extended families and our friends. Please abide with us, relieve any of anxiety and direct our ways. Thank you for your leniency regarding our trials. I pray for your continued help and for deliverance from them, for deliverance from my sinful nature, from the evils of the world, and the evil one. Please protect our homes, our vehicles, our work places, our church facilities, our work, our activities and our travels, our bodies, minds, spirits and emotions; please drive the evil one and his emissaries away in the name and by the power of the blood of Jesus.

This is one and obviously very personal example of how the Lord's Prayer may serve as a guide and model both in content and order for private praying. Certainly we might pray one of the phrases of the Lord's Prayer, and then amplify extemporaneously, as in the rabbinic tradition. In light of these potentialities, we may say the prayer not only has *unifying, confessional, educational* and *transmissional* import, it also has *devotional* value.

The Lord's Prayer also possesses *ethical* value. As with the Ten Commandments which may be divided into two sections, four words about devotion to God and six words dealing with appropriate human relations, so also in the Lord's Prayer are given two areas of concern, allegiance to God and duty to others. Max Lucado, in his creative volume mentioned in the introduction of this study, wrote: "In these verses Christ has provided more than a model for prayer, he has provided a model for living."[238] We have the right to pray for protection from evil and the Evil One; we also have the responsibility to live in a manner which guards against influencing others in wrong ways. We have the right to pray for forgiveness of sins; but we also have the responsibility to forgive others. Not only are we given the right to petition God for

---

[238] Lucado, 5.

bread; we are given also the responsibility to help others acquire their basic needs. We have the right and privilege to enter God's kingdom. We are also given the responsibility to increase in the kingdom and do God's will, and to help others enter and increase and do God's will as well. We have the right to call upon God. We have the responsibility to honor God's name and reputation. We have the privilege of praying the Lord's Prayer together with other Christians. We have the responsibility to so live that we preserve the unity of the Christian witness. These are some of the ethical implications and values of the prayer.

We may say the Lord's Prayer also has *symbolic* value. As we have stated previously, praying the Lord's Prayer is a mark of identity and allegiance. Praying the prayer in the assembly is a group sign to others that we desire to be known as Christian. In another way, it may be fair to say that praying it has become for Christians a kind of *sacramental event*. We may think of its use as a thing-event through which we are brought into the presence of a holy God and place ourselves in a position of receiving God's grace. Praying the prayer may be viewed as a *door to the sacred*.[239] Indeed, Cyprian and Augustine spoke of the sacramentality of the phrases of the Lord's Prayer.[240]

Many times we have difficulty finding the right words to express the inexpressible. Praying the Lord's Prayer helps us in those times when all other words fail. It says more than we could ever say, even when we are not thoroughly cognitive of the significance of each phrase. The prayer says more than it means. It represents something greater and loftier and more profound than our words could ever convey. It symbolizes all of the deepest longings of our hearts.

Conclusion

From the above we see that praying the Lord's Prayer in corporate worship especially, as well as in private devotions, has many values and

---

[239] Macquarrie, 14.

[240] Cyprian. Treatise IV, "On the Lord's Prayer," *Ante-Nicene Fathers*, Vol. 5, 449 (and note); Augustine is cited in Stevenson, *The Lord's Prayer: A Text in Tradition*, 84.

potentialities. Praying together cultivates *unity* as the body of Christ and enhances communion with God. As a kingdom of priests to the world, we have the obligation to band together and become mature ambassadors (Jn. 17:20-23, Eph. 4:13). Praying the Lord's Prayer together assists in nurturing the sense of oneness and togetherness we have by faith in Christ. This is a unity evermore needed in a world which seems bent on promoting values which only lead to the fracturing of families and the stifling of the discussion of religious values in public discourse. We must do all we can as Christians to foster wholeness, unity, harmony, and spiritual maturity. The study and intentional and sensible use of the Lord's Prayer in worship in particular is one ingredient in God's program for cultivating these qualities. Thanks be to God.

Review Guide

Introduction

1. List the descriptions for the Lord's Prayer given by various authors.

2. What does each one tell us about the prayer?

3. What do they have in common?

4. How are they different?

Overview

1. Write out both versions of the Lord's Prayer (Matthew 6:9-13, Luke 11:2-4). Describe how they compare.

2. The Sermon on the Mount in Matthew's version is the scriptural context of the prayer. What are some of the significances for the inclusion of the Lord's Prayer based on the labels others have given to the Sermon on the Mount?

3. What is Jesus' overall purpose for presenting the commentary on the three essential Jewish acts of righteousness?

4. In your own words describe what are the categories of the inclusions of the prayer.

5. In what order has Jesus offered the inclusions?

Jewish Setting

1. Describe the *intention* of Jesus' teaching a prayer to/for the disciples.

2. Look up some of the citations which illustrate the *content* of the phrases of the Lord's Prayer are reflective of Old Testament Jewish thought.

3. With what other Old Testament passages does the Lord's Prayer have a correspondence regarding *shape* and *direction of thought*?

4. What is the significance of the *Talmud* for appreciating the Jewish setting of the Lord's Prayer?

5. Describe the similarities between the *Kaddish* and the Lord's Prayer.

6. In what ways is the Lord's Prayer similar to the *Amidah*?

7. Summarize/list the various aspects of the Jewish setting of the Lord's Prayer.

Addressing God

1. Why did Jesus say the term *Father* is the appropriate way to address God in prayer?

2. What do *Father* and *in heaven* tell us about the nature of the one addressed?

3. In what ways may we say God is our Father?

Hallowing God's Name

1. What are the meanings of *hallow* and *holy*?

2. What is the significance of the name of God?

3. How do we hallow God's name?

Entering the Kingdom of God

1. What are the two dimensions of God's kingdom?

2. What does *kingdom of God* mean?

3. What does the *nearness* of the kingdom mean?

4. What are the two *kinds* of God's kingdom?

5. What is the present reality of God's kingdom called?

Review Guide

6. What is the future realm of God's kingdom called?

7. How do persons enter the kingdom of God's grace?

8. What is the requirement for entry?

9. What does *come* mean?

10. What does the term *come* imply?

Increasing in the Kingdom of God

1. What are several reasons why Christians are expected to increase in the kingdom of God's grace? List the accompanying scriptures.

2. What are various methods by which Christians may increase in the kingdom?

3. What are a number of values of increasing?

Imagining the Kingdom of God's Glory

1. What are the meanings of the Bible terms for *glory*?

2. What are some of the biblical images for the kingdom of God's glory?

3. What does the term *heaven* suggest?

4. What does *going to heaven* mean?

5. What do the descriptions of the Holy City tell us about the New Jerusalem?

Passing into the Kingdom of God's Glory

1. What are the biblical terms for the realm of departed spirits?

2. What does the account of the afterlife of the rich man and Lazarus (Luke 16:19-31) suggest about the time between this life and the resurrection?

3. Write a brief paragraph summarizing the events of Jesus' second coming.

4. What steps should be taken to ease the sting of facing death?

Doing God's Will

1. What is the aspect of God's will which speaks of the plan of God being carried out and completed?

2. What is the aspect of God's will which refers to people keeping his commands, decrees and ordinances?

3. What is meant by God's personal will and what are its three components?

4. How is the will of God accomplished in heaven?

5. Based on Psalm 103:19-21, what do we learn are included in the three-fold doing of God's will by the angels?

6. List the ways God's will is done by the angels, and provide their accompanying scriptures.

Requesting Daily Provisions

1. In what ways have some interpreters viewed the term *bread*?

2. As a figure of speech, what is the intended meaning of *bread* as it is used in the petition?

3. What does C. F. Yoder's translation of bread as a *little loaf* emphasize?

4. What does God's supply of our daily provisions demonstrate?

5. What two things do the terms *this day* and *daily* suggest?

Seeking Forgiveness of Sins

1. What are the three English terms for *sin* found either in the body of the Lord's Prayer or in Jesus' added commentary?

2. To what is sin likened?

3. What does the term for sin in the added commentary literally mean?

4. What does the term for sin in Luke's account mean?

5. List and describe the four ingredients of repentance.

6. How is the initial turn to God made?

Forgiving Others

1. What is the main focus of the fifth petition?

2. What is the condition of God's conferring on-going forgiveness?

3. What does the term *as* mean in the petition?

4. List reasons for forgiving and provide accompanying scriptures.

Praying for Leniency

1. What does the New Testament term traditionally rendered *temptation* mean?

2. For what does Jesus permit us to pray in the first half of this petition?

3. What is the focus of praying *Lead us not into temptation*?

4. List reasons why God allows testing.

Pleading for Deliverance

1. How does the apostle Paul refer to the evil within our hearts?

2. Give three terms for the evil one and define them.

3. What does the word *deliver* in the prayer mean?

4. How may the second clause of the petition be understood?

5. How may Christians counter and combat the attacks of the evil one?

Praising God

1. In the traditional praying of the Lord's Prayer, what is the meaning of the closing statement?

2. What is its function in the prayer?

3. What is the meaning and purpose of the concluding *Amen*?

Summarizing the Prayer

1. From the summaries given, list many Christian beliefs which are encapsulated in the Lord's Prayer.

Praying the Lord's Prayer

1. What in the prayer indicates it was intended for group use?

2. What are several values for praying the Lord's Prayer in corporate worship?

3. How may the Lord's Prayer help shape private prayers?

4. As with an index prayer in the rabbinic tradition, write your own prayer, first giving a phrase from the Lord's Prayer, then expanding it in your own words.

Bibliography

Aquinas, St. Thomas. *Summa Theologiae*. Vol. 39. New York: McGraw-Hill Book Company, 1964.

Appleton, George, ed. *The Oxford Book of Prayer*. New York: Oxford University Press, 1985.

Augustine. "Our Lord's Sermon on the Mount." *Nicene and Post-Nicene Fathers*. Vol. 6. Philip Schaff, ed. Peabody, Mass: Hendrickson Publishers, 1994.

Ayo, Nicolas. *The Lord's Prayer: A Survey Theological and Literary*. Notre Dame: University of Notre Dame Press, 1992.

Backhouse, Robert, comp. *1500 Illustrations for Preaching & Teaching*. London: Marshall Pickering, 1991.

Bainton, Roland. *Here I Stand: A Life of Martin Luther*. New York: Mentor Books, New American Library, 995.

Barclay, William. *The Gospel of Luke*, rev. ed. Philadelphia: The Westminster Press, 1975.

_____. *The Gospel of Matthew*. Vol. 1, rev. ed. Philadelphia: The Westminster Press, 1975.

_____. *The Gospel of Matthew*. Vol. 2, rev. ed. Philadelphia: The Westminster Press, 1975.

_____. *The Lord's Prayer*. Louisville: Westminster John Knox Press, 1998.

_____. *The Revelation of John*, rev. ed. Philadelphia: The Westminster Press, 1976.

Barth, Karl. *Evangelical Theology: An Introduction*. Grand Rapids: William B. Eerdmans Publishing Company, 1963.

_____. *Prayer*, sec. ed. Philadelphia: The Westminster Press, 1985.

Baxter, Richard. *A Call to the Unconverted*. Portsmouth, New Hampshire: John Melcher, 1795.

Benson, Louis F. *The Hymnody of the Christian Church.* Richmond: John Knox Press, 1956.

Best, Thomas F. and Heller, Dagmar, eds. *So We Believe, So We Pray.* Geneva: WCC Publications, 1995.

Bommer Josef. "The Lord's Prayer in Pastoral Usage." *The Lord's Prayer and Jewish Liturgy.* edited by Jakob Petcuchowski and Michael Brocke: New York: Seabury Press, 1978.

Bonhoeffer, Dietrich. *Letters and Papers From Prison.* New York: MacMillan, 1953.

_____. *The Cost of Discipleship.* New York: The Macmillan Company, 1970.

Brown, R. E. "The Pater Noster as an Eschatological Prayer," *New Testament Essays.* New York: Doubleday, 1982.

Brown, Robert McAfee. *The Ecumenical Revolution.* Garden City, New York: Doubleday & Company, Inc. 1967.

Cairns, Alan. *The Lord's Prayer.* Greenville, SC: Ambassador International, 2004.

Calvin, John. "Commentary and Harmony of the Evangelists." *Calvin's Commentaries.* Vol. XVI. Grand Rapids: Baker Book House, 1993.

_____. "Commentaries on the Four Last Books of Moses Arranged in the Form of a Harmony." Volume Second. *Calvin's Commentaries.* Volume II. Grand Rapids: Baker Book House, 1993.

_____. *Institutes of the Christian Religion.* edited by John T. McNeil. Philadelphia: Westminster Press, 1960.

Carmignac, Jean. "The Spiritual Wealth of the Lord's Prayer." *The Lord's Prayer and Jewish Liturgy,* edited by Jakob Petuchowski and Michael Brocke. New York: Seabury Press, 1978.

Carson, D. A. *Jesus' Sermon on the Mount (And His Confrontation with the World).* Grand Rapids: Baker Book House, 2005.

Central Board of Finance of the Church of England. *The Alternative Service Book 1980.* Colchester: William Clowes Ltd, 1980.

Charlesworth, James H. "Jewish Prayers in the Time of Jesus." *Princeton Seminary Bulletin* Supplement 2 (1992): 36-55.

Bibliography

Charlesworth, James H., ed. *The Lord's Prayer and Other Prayer Texts From the Greco-Roman Era*. Valley Forge: Trinity Press International, 1994.

Chemnitz, Martin. *The Lord's Prayer*. St. Louis: Concordia Publishing House, 1999.

Chrysostom. "Homilies of the Gospel of Saint Matthew." *Nicene and Post-Nicene Fathers*. Vol. 10. Philip Schaff, ed. Peabody, Mass: Hendrickson Publishers, 1994.

Clark, Linda J. *Music in Churches*. Bethseda, Maryland: Alban Institute, 1994.

Clendenin, Daniel B. "What the Orthodox Believe." *Christian History*. Issue 54 (1997): 32-35.

Coggan, Donald. *The Prayers of the New Testament*. London: Hodder & Stoughton, 1967.

Consultation on Common Texts. *The Revised Common Lectionary*. Nashville: Abingdon Press, 1992.

Courtier, Paul. "Prayer and Christian Unity." *The Ecumenical Movement: An Anthology of Key Texts and Voices*, edited by Michael Kinnamon and Brian Cope. Geneva: WCC Publications, 1997.

Cross, F. L., ed. *The Oxford Dictionary of the Christian Church*. London: Oxford University Press, 1957.

Cyprian. "Elucidations III." *Ante-Nicene Fathers*. Vol. 5, edited by Alexander Roberts and James Donaldson. Peabody, Mass: Hendrickson Publishers, 1994.

_____. "On the Lord's Prayer" [Treatise IV]. *Ante-Nicene Fathers*. Vol. 5, ed. by Alexander Roberts and James Donaldson. Peabody Mass: Hendrickson Publisher's, 1994.

Cyril of Jerusalem. "The Catechetical Lectures" XXIII, 15. *Nicene and Post-Nicene Fathers*. Second Series, Vol. 7. Peabody, Mass: Hendrickson Publishers, 1994.

Davies, W. D. & Allison, Dale C. Jr. *The Gospel According to St. Matthew*, Vol. I (Critical and Exegetical Commentary Series). Edinburgh: T. & T. Clark, 1988.

Dearmer, Percy, ed. *The English Hymnal With Tunes 1933*. London: Oxford University Press, 1933.

Deissler, Alfons. "The Spirit of the Lord's Prayer in the Faith and Worship of the Old Testament." *The Lord's Prayer and Jewish Liturgy*, ed. by Jakob Petuchowski and Michael Brocke. New York: Seabury Press, 1978.

Denny, Randal. *The Kingdom, The Power, The Glory: Embracing the Mystery of the Lord's Prayer*. Kansas City, Missouri: Beacon Hill Press, 1997.

Di Berardino, Angelo, ed. *Patrology*. trans. by Rev. Placid Solari. Westminster, Maryland: Christian Classics, Inc., 1986.

Dodd, Brian J. *Praying Jesus' Way: A Guide for Beginners and Veterans*. Downers Grove, Illinois: InterVarsity Press, 1997.

Dyck, Arthur. *Rethinking Rights and Responsibilities: The Moral Bonds of Community*. Cleveland: The Pilgrim Press, 1994.

Dulles, Avery. *Models of the Church*. expanded edition. New York: Doubleday, 1987.

Edwards, Jonathan. "Sinners in the Hands of an Angry God." *The Works of Jonathan Edwards*, Volume Two. Edinburgh: The Banner of Truth Trust, 1986.

Ellens, J. Harold. "Communication Theory and Petitionary Prayer." *Journal of Psychology and Theology* 5, no. 1 (1977): 48-54.

Ellison, H. L. *Exodus*. Philadelphia: The Westminster Press, 1982.

English Language Liturgical Consultation. *Praying Together*. Nashville: Abingdon Press, 1988.

Eskew, Harry and McElrath, Hugh T. *Sing With Understanding: An Introduction to Christian Hymnology*. Nashville: Church Street Press, 1995.

Evans, Tony. *Tony Evans Speaks Out on Prayer*. Chicago: Moody Press, 2000.

Feldman, Edmund Burke. *Varieties of Visual Experience*. Englewood Cliffs, New Jersey: Prentice-Hall, 1967.

Fitzgerald, Thomas. "Unity and Prayer." *So We Believe, So We Pray*, edited by Thomas Best and Dagmar Heller. Geneva: WCC Publications, 1995.

Fleming, William. *Arts and Ideas*, third ed. New York: Holt, Rinehart & Winston, Inc., n.d.

Flynn, Leslie B. *The Master's Plan of Prayer*. Grand Rapids: Kregel Publications, 1995.

Bibliography

Goulder, M. D. "The Composition of the Lord's Prayer." *Journal of Theological Studies* (1963): 32-45.

Grant, John Webster. "The Hymn as Theological Statement." *The Hymn*. 37, no. 4 (October 1986): 7-10.

Hamilton, Dan. *Forgiveness*. Downers Grove, Illinois: InterVarsity Press, 1980.

Hanson, Paul. *The People Called: The Growth of Community in the Bible*. San Francisco: Harper & Row Publishers, 1986.

Harner, P. B. *Understanding the Lord's Prayer*. Philadelphia: Fortress Press, 1975.

Hauerwas, Stanley and Willimon, William. *Resident Aliens: Life in the Christian Colony*. Nashville: Abingdon Press, 1989.

Hemphill, Ken. *The Prayer of Jesus*. Nashville: Broadman & Holman Publishers, 2001.

Henry, Matthew. *A Method for Prayer*. Fearn, Scotland: Christian Focus Publications Ltd, 1994.

_____. *Matthew Henry's Commentary On the Whole Bible*. Vol. 5. Peabody Mass: Hendrickson Publications, 1996.

_____. *The Pleasantness of a Religious Life*. Morgan, Penn: Soli Deo Gloria Publications, 1996.

_____. *The Secret of Communion With God*. Grand Rapids: Kregel Publications, 1991.

Hesselink, I. John. *Calvin's First Catechism. A Commentary*. Louisville, Kentucky: Westminster John Knox Press, 1997.

Hildebrandt, Franz and Beckerlegge, Oliver A., eds. *The Works of John Wesley. Volume 7: A Collection of Hymns for use of the People called Methodists*. Oxford: Clarendon Press, 1983.

Hoffman, Rabbi Lawrence A., ed. *The Amidah*. Vol. 2 of *My People's Prayer Book: Traditional Prayers, Modern Commentaries*. Woodstock, Vermont: Jewish Lights Publishing, 2003.

Hughes, R. Kent. *ABBA Father: The Lord's Pattern for Prayer*. Wheaton, IL: Crossway Books, 1986.

International Consultation on English Texts. *Prayers We Have in Common*. Philadelphia: Fortress Press, 1975.

Janzow, F. Samuel. *Luther's Large Catechism*. St. Louis: Concordia Publishing House, 1978.

Jeremiah, David. *Prayer The Great Adventure*. Sisters, Oregon: Multnomah Publishers, Inc., 1997.

Jeremias, Joachim. *Abba: Stidien zur neutestamentlichen Theologie und Zeitgeschichte*. Gottingen: Vandenhoeck & Ruprecht, 1966.

———. *The Lord's Prayer*. J. Reumann, ed. et trans. Philadelphia: Fortress Press, 1980.

———. *The Prayers of Jesus*. Studies in Biblical Theology 2, no. 6 London: SCM Press, 1967.

Jochum, Herbert. "Teaching the Lord's Prayer." *The Lord's Prayer and Jewish Liturgy*, edited by Jakob Petuchowski and Michael Brocke. New York: Seabury Press, 1978.

John Paul II. *Ut Urum Sint: Encyclical on Commitment to Ecumenism*. Vatican City: Liberia Editrice Vaticana, 1995.

Kavanagh, Aidan. *On Liturgical Theology*. New York: Pueblo Publishing Company, 1984.

Kimbrough, Jr. S. T. "Hymns Are Theology." *Theology Today*. XLII, no. 1 (April 1985): 59-68.

Kisley, Lorraine. *The Prayer of Fire: Experiencing the Lord's Prayer*. Brewster, Mass: Paraclete Press, 2004.

Knight, George A. F. *Leviticus*. Philadelphia: The Westminster Press, 1981.

Lathop, Gordon. "Knowing Something a Little: On the Role of the Lex Orandi in the Search for Christian Unity." *So We Believe, So We Pray*, edited by Thomas Best and Dagmar Heller. Geneva: WCC Publications, 1995.

Layman, Charles M. *The Lord's Prayer In Its Biblical Setting*. Nashville: Abingdon Press, 1968.

Leaver, Robin. *Catherine Winkworth: The Influence of Her Translations on English Hymnody*. St. Louis: Concordia Publishing House, 1978.

———. "The Hymnbook as a Book of Practical Theology." *Reformed Liturgy and Music*. XXIV, no. 2 (Spring 1990): 55-57.

Bibliography

Lewis, Peter. *On Our Knees and In His Arms: The Lord's Prayer*. Chicago: Moody Press, 1998.

Lloyd-Jones, D. Martyn. *Studies in the Sermon on the Mount* (in Two Volumes). Grand Rapids: Wm. B. Eerdmans Publishing Company, 1996.

Lochman, Jan Milic. *The Lord's Prayer*, G. W. Bromiley, ed. et trans. Grand Rapids: Wm. B. Eerdmans Publishing Company, 1990.

Lohmeyer, Ernest. *Our Father: An Introduction to the Lord's Prayer*. New York: Harper & Row, Publishers, 1965.

Lucado, Max. *The Great House of God*. Dallas: Word Publishing, 1997.

Luther, Martin. "Lectures on Genesis." *Luther's Works*. Vol. 2. Jaroslav Pelikan, ed. St. Louis: Concordia Publishing House, 1960.

_____. "Ten Sermons on the Catechism, 1528." *Luther's Works*. Vol. 51, John W. Doberstein, ed. & trans. Philadelphia: Fortress Press, 1959.

_____. "The Sermon on the Mount: Sermons." *Luther's Works*. Vol. 21, Jaroslav Pelikan, ed. St. Louis: Concordia Publishing House, 1956.

Macquarrie, John. *A Guide to the Sacraments*. New York: Continuum, 1997.

McBrien, Richard P. *Catholicism*. Minneapolis: Winston Press Inc., 1981.

McElrath, Hugh T. "The Hymnbook as a Compendium of Theology." *Review and Expositor*. Vol. 87, no. 1 (Winter 1990): 11-31.

Meeks, Wayne A. *The Origins of Christian Morality: The First Two Centuries*. New Haven: Yale University Press, 1993.

Miller, J. Allen. *Christian Doctrine: Lectures and Sermons*. Ashland, Ohio: The Brethren Publishing Company, 1946.

Miller, S. Madeleine and Miller, J. Lane. *Harper's Bible Dictionary*. New York: Harper and Row, Publishers, 1973.

Morgan, Edmund S., ed. *Puritan Political Ideas* 1558-1794. Indianapolis: Bibbs-Merrill, 1995.

Morgan, G. Campbell. *The Practice of Prayer*. Belfast, Northern Ireland: Ambassador Productions, LTD, 1965.

Mullholland, James. *Praying Like Jesus: The Lord's Prayer in a Culture of Prosperity*. SanFrancisco: HarperSanFrancisco, 2001.

Murray, Andrew. *With Christ in the School of Prayer.* Springdale, Penn: Whitaker House, 1981.

Nee, Watchman. *The Prayer Ministry of the Church.* Anaheim, CA: Living Stream Ministry, 1993.

Oesterley, W. O. E. *The Jewish Background of the Christian Liturgy.* Oxford: Clarendon Press, 1925.

Osborn, G. *The Poetical Works of John and Charles Wesley.* Vol. X. London: Wesleyan-Methodist Conference Office, 1871.

Petuchowski, Jakob J. & Brocke, Michael, ed. *The Lord's Prayer and Jewish Liturgy.* New York: Seabury Press, 1978.

Pink, Arthur W. *An Exposition of the Sermon on the Mount.* Grand Rapids: Kregel Publications, 1986.

Pope Pius XII. *Mediator Dei: Encyclical Letter on the Sacred Liturgy.* Washington, D.C. : National Catholic Welfare Conference, 1947.

Powell, Ivor. *Matthew's Majestic Gospel.* Grand Rapids: Kregel Publications, 1986.

Presbyterian Hymnal. Louisville, Kentucky: Westminster/John Knox, 1990.

Rahner, Karl, ed. Sacramentum Mundi: *An Encyclopedia of Theology.* Vol. 3. New York: Herder & Herder, 1969.

Rattenbury, J. Ernest. *The Evangelical Doctrines of Charles Wesley's Hymns.* London: The Epworth Press, 1941.

Robinson, Haddon. *Jesus' Blueprint for Prayer.* Grand Rapids: RBC Ministries, 1989.

Roussakis, Peter E. *Confessing the Compendium: Praying the Lord's Prayer as Confessing Faith.* Burlington, IN: Meetinghouse Press, 2005.

Routley, Erik. "Amen and Christian Liturgy." *Reformed Liturgy and Music.* Vol. XIII, no. 1 (Winter 1979): 19-23.

Ryken, Philip Graham. *When You Pray: Making the Lord's Prayer Your Own.* Wheaton, Illinois: Crossway Books, 2000.

Sampley, J. Paul. *Walking Between the Times: Paul's Moral Reasoning.* Minneapolis: Fortress Press, 1991.

Bibliography

Saphir, Adolph. *Our Lord's Pattern of Prayer*. Grand Rapids: Kregel Publications, 1984.

Schaff, Philip. *A Christian Catechism for Sunday Schools and Families*. Philadelphia: American Sunday School Union, 1880.

Schaff, Philip and Schaff, Rev. David S., eds. *The Creeds of Christendom* (Three Volumes). Grand Rapids: Baker Book House, 1993.

Schilling, S. Paul. *The Faith We Sing: How the Message of Hymns Can Enhance Christian Belief*. Philadelphia: The Westminster Press, 1983.

Schumann, Heinz. *Praying With Christ*. New York: Herder & Herder, 1964.

Segler, Franklin M. *Christian Worship: Its Theology and Practice*. Nashville: Broadman Press, 1967.

Shurer, Emil. *A History of the Jewish People in the Time of Jesus Christ*. Second Division, Vol. II. Peabody, Mass: Hendrickson Publishers, 1995.

Simon, Art. *Rediscovering the Lord's Prayer*. Minneapolis: Augsburg Books, 2005.

Sponheim, Paul R. ed. *A Primer on Prayer*. Philadelphia: Fortress Press, 1988.

Spring, Gardiner. *The Mercy Seat: Thoughts Suggested by the Lord's Prayer*. Morgan, PA: Soli Deo Gloria Publications, 2001.

Stagg, Frank. "Matthew." *The Broadman Bible Commentary* Volume 8. Nashville: Broadman Press, 1969.

Stevenson, Kenneth. *Abba Father: Understanding and Using the Lord's Prayer*. Harrisburg, Penn: Morehouse Publishing, 2000.

Stevenson, Kenneth W. *The Lord's Prayer: A Text in Tradition*. Minneapolis: Fortress Press, 2004.

Stott, John R. W. *The Message of the Sermon on the Mount*. Downers Grove, IL: Inter-Varsity Press, 1978.

TANAKH. *The Holy Scriptures: The New JPS Translation According to the Traditional Hebrew Text*. Philadelphia: The Jewish Publication Society, 1985.

Tertullian. "On Prayer." *Ante-Nicene Fathers*. Vol. 3. Alexander Roberts & James Donaldson, eds. Trans. by Rev. S. Thelwall. Peabody, Mass: Hendrickson Publishers, 1994.

The New Century Hymnal. Cleveland, Ohio: The Pilgrim Press, 1995.

The United Methodist Book of Worship. Nashville: The United Methodist Publishing House, 1992.

Thielicke, Helmut. *Our Heavenly Father: Sermons on the Lord's Prayer.* John W. Doberstein, trans. New York: Harper & Row, Publishers, 1960.

Tixeront, Joseph. *A Handbook of Patrology.* London: B. Herder Book Co., 1943.

Towns, Elmer L. *Praying and the Lord's Prayer.* Ventura, CA: Regal Books, 1977.

Trueblood, Elton. *The Lord's Prayer.* New York: Harper & Row Publishers, 1965.

Underhill, Evelyn. *Abba: Meditations Based on the Lord's Prayer.* London: Longmans, 1940.

United States Catholic Conference. *Catechism of the Catholic Church.* Vatican City: Liberia Editrice Vaticana, 1994.

Vincent, Nathaniel. "The Conversion of a Sinner," *The Puritans on Conversion,* Don Kistler, ed. Morgan, Penn: Soli Deo Gloria Publications, 1990.

Vine, W. E. *An Expository Dictionary of New Testament Words.* Nashville: Thomas Nelson, Publishers, 1952.

Wainwright, Geoffrey. *Doxology: The Praise of God in Worship, Doctrine and Life. A Systematic Theology.* New York: Oxford University Press, 1980.

Watson, Thomas. *The Lord's Prayer.* Edinburgh: The Banner of Truth Trust, 1993.

Weil, Louis. *Gathered to Pray: Understanding Liturgical Prayer.* Cambridge, Mass: Cowley Publications, 1986.

Wesley, John. "Upon Our Lord's Sermon on the Mount," Sermon XXVI, Discourse VI. *The Works of John Wesley,* Third Edition, Vol. V. Grand Rapids: Baker Book House, 1991.

Willimon, William H. *Worship as Pastoral Care.* Nashville: Abingdon Press, 1979.

Willimon, William H. and Hauerwas, Stanley. *Lord, Teach Us: The Lord's Prayer and the Christian Life.* Nashville: Abingdon Press, 1996.

Witsius, Herman. *Sacred Dissertations on The Lord's Prayer.* Escondido, California: The den Dulk Christian Foundation, 1994.

Bibliography

Wright, N. T. *The Lord and His Prayer*. Grand Rapids: William B. Eerdmans Publishing Company, 1996.

Wuest, Kenneth S. *The New Testament: An Expanded Translation*. Grand Rapids: Wm. B. Eerdmans Publishing Company, 1994.

Yoder, C. F. *God's Means of Grace*. Elgin, Illinois: Brethren Publishing House, 1908.

Young, Frances. *The Making of Creeds*. London: SCM Press, 1991.

Young, Brad H. *The Jewish Background to the Lord's Prayer*. Austin, Texas: Center for Judaic-Christian Studies, 1984.

Youssef, Michael. *The Prayer That God Answers: Experiencing the Power and Fullness of The Lord's Prayer*. Nashville: Thomas Nelson Publishers, 2000.

Zacharias, Ravi. *Deliver Us From Evil: Restoring the Soul in a Disintegrating Culture*. Dallas: Word Publishing, 1996.

Index

Abba, 28
addereth, 62
adopted/adoption, 29
aion, 83
Amen, 156, 165
Amidah, 18 [& note], 20, 22
anomia, 112
aphiemi, 118
artos, 103-104
ascription of praise, 151, 158, 165
Aquinas, Thomas (c. 1225-1274), 1
Augustine (354-430), 39 [note], 46, 101, 178
Ayo, Nicolas, 1, 3

Barclay, William (1907-1978), 4, 12, 15, 30, 107, 123
Barth, Karl (1886-1968), 3, 40-41 [the prayer], 111, 147
basileia, he basileai sou, 44, 50
Beatitudes, 9, 16, 24
Baalzebub, beelzebub, 147
benedictions [*berakoth*], blessings, 16 [note], 20
birth of the spirit, 49
body of divinity [Watson], 1-2
Bommer, Josef, 4
Bonhoeffer, Dietrich (1906-1945), 176
Book of Common Prayer (1662), 130
bread, 12, 21, 101-108, 162
breviarium totius evangelii [Tertullian], 2
brief formula [Luther], 2
brief summary of the doctrine of Christ [Calvin], 9
Brocke, Michael, 4

Calvin, John (1509-1564), 1, 4, 9, 34, 27-38, 48-49, 94-95, 105, 123
canonical prayer [Stevenson], 16, 23
Carmignac, Jean, 4
Charlesworth, James, 4
come [as in *Thy kingdom come*], 44, 48, 50, 159

compendium of the whole gospel [Tertullian], 2 [& note], 23, 174-175
compendium of Christ's doctrine, 9
comprehension, 114-116, 121
comprehensive and sublime compend [Cyprian], 2
comprehensiveness, 130
condition [of on-going forgiveness], 122-123, 163
confession, 114-116, 121
confessional import/potentiality/value [Ellens, Roussakis], 174 [& note], 175, 177
contemporary need, 130
contrition, 114-116, 121
conversion, convert, 114-116, 122
creation, 28 [& note], 29
curriculum for prayer [Youssef], 170
Cyprian (200-258), 2, 178
Cyril of Jerusalem (c. 315-386), 126

daily, 101, 105-106
debtors, debts, 110-115, 130-131, 162-163
declaratory profession of faith in petitionary formula [Ellens], 172
deliver, deliverance, 141-150 (esp. 147-148)
De Oratione (On Prayer), 2
devil, 145, 164
devotional value, 177
diabolos, 145
Didache, 22, 152
digest of doctrine [Luther], 2, 175
directory for prayer [Watson], 1
distillation of the good news [Ayo], 3
Dodd, Brian, 5
door to the sacred [Macquarrie], 178
doxa, dokeo, doxazo, 62
doxological summary [Ellens], 172
doxology, 22, 62, 151-155, 165
Dyck, Arthur, 98

educational value, 174-175, 177
El, 34-36, 39
election, 29

Index

Eighteen Benedictions (Shemone Esre Berakoth), 20
Ellens, J. Harold, 4, 172
Ellucidations III [Cyprian], 2 [note]
eltheto, 50
encapsulation/embodiment of Christian belief [Roussakis], viii, 3, 171
epiousion, 105
epitome of the whole gospel [Tertullian/Thelwell], 2 [note]
ethical value, 177
Eucharist, 102
evil from within [sinful nature], 142-143, 148, 164
evil of the world, 133, 143-144, 164
Evil One, 134-150 (esp. 144-147), 164

Father, 15, 21, 25 [& note], 26-31, 34, 158
floor plan to our spiritual house [Lucado], 2
forgiveness/forgiving, 121-129, 162-163

gehenna, 73 [& note], 77
Gloria Patri, 62, 154
glory, 61-63, 153
Golden Rule, 9
gospel antidote [Watson], 69
gospel in a nutshell [Schaff], 3, 175
Graham, Billy, 117

hadar, 62
hades, 73-74, 77
hagios, hagiazesthai, 33
hallelu, hallelujah, 35
hallow, hallowed, 21, 33-41
hamartias, 112, 131
Hauerwas, Stanley, 3
heaven, heavens, 27, 34, 63-66
hell, 72 [note], 73 [& note], 74 [note], 77
Henry, Matthew (1662-1714), 2, 4, 37, 86, 95, 153
hodh, 62
Holy City, 63, 66-69

imperatives, 93, 99-100
inclusions, 11-12, 157-166
index prayer, 175
interdependence, interdependent, 97

Jeremiah, David, 2, 5, 40, 135
Jewish setting, 15-24 [& notes]
Jochum, Herbert, 4
Jones, D. Martyn-Lloyd (1899-1981), 125, 142

kabodh, 62
Kaddish, Half-Kaddish, 18 [& note], 19 [& note], 20, 22-23
kerygma, 174 [& note]
keynote of all Christian prayers [Schaff], 171
kingdom, kingdom of God, 23, 43-69, 159-160
kingdom of God's glory [Watson], 46-47, 61-79, 159
kingdom of God's grace [Watson], 46-59, 112, 159

leniency, lenient, 136, 139, 164
lightbearer, 146
limitation, 105, 107, 162
Lucado, Max, 2, 5, 177
Lucifer, 146
Luther, Martin (1483-1546), 1-2, 7-9, 11 [note], 36, 39, 49, 106-107 [poem
  & note], 128, 142-145, 147, 149, 158 [& note], 159-160, 162-163, 165, 175

Magna Charta of the Kingdom, 9
Manifesto of the King, 3, 9
manner of doing God's will, 87-90, 160
mark of identity, 15, 23, 169, 178
mature, 55
method for praying [Henry], 2
Millenium, 76-77
Miller, J. Allen (1866-1935), 73, 74 [& note]
mini-encyclopedia of Christian belief, viii
minimum, 104-105, 107, 162
Mishnah, 17 [note]
model prayer [Stagg], 2, 175
Montgomery, James (1771-1854), 8

Index

Moody, Dwight L. (1837-1899), 129
Morgan, G. Campbell (1863-1945), 2-3, 17, 123-124, 175
morning star, 146
mutual dependence, 97

name, names [for God], 21, 34-36
New Jerusalem, 63, 66-69

Old, Hughes Oliphant, 22
opheilemata, ophleilonti, 110-112
order, 12-13
ordination address, 9
ouranos, ouranois, 27, 65
outline for prayer, 1

paradise, 74, 79
parabasis, 112
paraptomata, 111-112
peirasmos, peirazein, 134
personal devotional orientation, 85-86
personal will, 85-86, 160
Petuchowski, Jakob, 4
Pink, Arthur (1886-1952), 153
plural, plurals, 96-97, 161-162
Powell, Ivor, 135
precis of the whole gospel [Ayo], 3
predestined will, 83-85, 160
preface, 13, 25-31, 151, 158
prerequisite, 47
prescribed form [Calvin], 1
prescribed will, 84, 86, 160
proclamation, proclaiming, 172-174
profanation, 36
progressive transformation, 54-55
protection, 133
public theology [Hauerwas & Willimon], 3
purity of intention [J. Wesley], 11

qualification, 97, 162

repentance, 113-119, 122
rescue, 147-148, 164
responsibility, 97-98
rhusai, 147
right of personal petition, 93-98
roadmap for prayer [Jeremiah], 2

sacramental event [Macquarrie], 178
sanctification, 54, 116
satan, 134-150, 164
Schaff, Philip (1819-1893), 3, 171, 175
sebhi, 62
second coming, 75-77
semeron, 105
Sermon on the Mount, 3, 9, 158
shamayim, 65
Shema, 16 [& note], 22-23
Shema and Its Blessings/Benedictions, 16 [& note], 20, 22
Shemone Esre Berakoth, 20
sheol, 72 [& note], 73-74
Similitudes, 9
sin, sins, 110-119, 130-131
sinful nature [evil within], 142-143, 148, 164
skene, 68
solemn address, 13
Stagg, Frank, 2, 4, 123
Stevenson, Kenneth, 5, 16, 19
Stott, John R.W. (1921-2011), 170, 176
strepho, 116
sudden change, 50
symbolic value, 178
synecdoche, 103, 162
system of divinity [Watson], 1-2

Talmud, 17 [& note], 18, 20
temptation, 133-136, 142, 164
Ten Commandments, 2, 13, 16, 94, 174, 177
tephillah, tefillah, 20 [& note], 93, 172

Index

Tertullian (c. 150-220), 2 [& note], 175
test, testing, 134-140, 142, 164
tetelestai, 115
thelema, 82
Thielicke, Helmut (1908-1986), 125, 154
this day, 101, 105-106
tohar, 62
Torah, 17 [note], 21
tou ponerou, 144
transmissional value, 175, 177
trespasses, 110, 129-130
Tyndale, William (c. 1490-1536), 129-130

unification, unifying, uniting, unity, viii, 8, 171, 174, 177, 179
unintentional sins, 112, 130
urgency, urgent, 99, 141, 148, 161

Wainwright, Geoffrey, 28
Watson, Thomas (1620-1688), 1-3, 40, 46, 48, 54, 69, 83, 89, 95, 104, 107, 123, 126-127, 142-144, 159-160
Wesley, Charles (1707-1788), 69, 128-129, 140
Wesley, John (1703-1791), 11, 39, 50, 58, 88, 102, 105, 126, 153-154
will [scope of God's], 82-86, 160
Willimon, William, 3
Witsius, Herman (1636-1708), 170-171
Wyrtzen, Jack, 117

Yah, Yahweh, 35, 39
Yoder, C. F. (1873-1955), 104
Youssef, Michael, 115

Zacharias, Ravi, 141, 143, 148

Biographical Note

Peter E. Roussakis
Ordained, The Brethren Church (Ashland, Ohio)

Education
BS, MS, Southern Connecticut State University
MCM, Southern Baptist Theological Seminary
STM, Boston University
DMin, Austin Presbyterian Theological Seminary
PhD, Graduate Theological Foundation

Service
Minister of Music (Kentucky, Ohio)
Pastor and Music Director (New Hampshire, Indiana)
Faculties: Ohio University, Ashland Theological Seminary (Ohio), Southwestern University (Texas), Granite State College (New Hampshire), Graduate Theological Foundation (Indiana)

www.ingramcontent.com/pod-product-compliance
Lightning Source LLC
Chambersburg PA
CBHW050147170426
43197CB00011B/1994